The People's Histo

Wallsend Shipyards

by

Andrew Clark and the
Wallsend People's Centre

Riverside fire fighters during the Second World War.

Copyright © Andrew Clark and the Wallsend People's Centre 1999

First published in 1999 by

The People's History Ltd
Suite 1
Byron House
Seaham Grange Business Park
Seaham
Co. Durham
SR7 0PY

ISBN 1 902527 53 4

Contents

Introduction   5

Acknowledgements   8

1.   Shipyard Life   9

2.   The Ships   45

3.   Working Conditions   59

4.   Women Workers   77

5.   Odd Tales   87

6.   The Save Our Swans Campaign   107

Introduction

This book has been a long term project for those involved and I am sure there are many who thought it would never see the light of day.

Stories were first collected by Durham University from women who had worked in the shipyards during the war. Further interviews were done by Tony Parker of the Wallsend People's Centre and Paul Bream and Val White of North Tyneside Libraries. The majority of these took place in 1993 and 1994 when the yard was in receivership and its future uncertain. Many of the stories reflect these troubled times. I have not changed the tone of these memories which are often tinged with bitterness of what was happening at that time. Many also thought that the end was about to come for this famous shipbuilding name.

The book starts with people's earliest memories of work and their first impressions before moving on to apprenticeships. First wage packets are still remembered as are the bowler-hatted gaffers and many former workmates. A common theme is how going into the yard was a family tradition and how the whole community was steeped in shipbuilding culture.

Some of the famous ships built on the Tyne are featured, including the *Mauretania, Esso Northumbria* and *Ark Royal*. These ships were often built while men suffered in terrible working conditions and it is important to show the hardships that were once common place in the yards. From the freezing cold to welder's fumes, workers had to endure

a harsh environment to get the job done. Accidents and the dangers of asbestos are recalled as well as the everyday discomforts of poor facilities.

It was important to include the contribution made by the many women who came to work in the yards during wartime. Bravely they faced the hard conditions with enthusiasm and humour to do their bit for the war effort. When peace came many were sad to return to their pre-war life.

Working in a shipyard seemed to develop a unique sense of humour and one section reflects the many characters, odd tales and jokes that were essential to lighten the day.

The final chapter of the book recalls the massive campaign which was launched when Swan Hunter's went into receivership in 1993. We end the book when HMS *Richmond* left the yard. For some that was the end of a chapter in the history of shipbuilding in the town.

I hope that the reader will appreciate that the memory can fade over many years and there may be a few of our story tellers who might have the odd fact mixed up. Please do not judge them too harshly. I also hope the reader doesn't mind that I occasionally nip out of Wallsend and include stories from other yards on the Tyne. So many men worked up and down the river it is a shame not to include memories of other yards.

As well as personal stories, I have used some newspaper articles and extracts from a few of the excellent books written about the industry. Also included is the poetry of Jack Davitt who as Ripyard Cuddling penned many a well-remembered verse. His poetry has the unique ability to capture what it was like to work in a shipyard with insight, imagination and humour.

The majority of the photographs have come from the archives of the Wallsend People's Centre. This archive is now being transferred on to computer to preserve this important historical record for future generations.

I am very grateful for the help given in the production of this book by the People's Centre. From the early days of the yard going into receivership the Centre gave its full support to the campaign to save Swan Hunter's – from producing banners and printing leaflets to helping to organise rallies and fund raising.

Since 1989 the Centre has claimed over £9 million pounds in benefits for ex-shipyard workers. It also offers advice and training for local people and is a popular meeting place for former workmates to reminisce about old times. Perhaps some of their stories are included in this book.

Andrew Clark
The People's History, 1999

Acknowledgements

The authors would like to thank the following who have assisted in the publication of this book. We are particularly grateful to all of those who have shared their memories of working in Wallsend shipyards:

Hugh Archibold, Allan Blackett, Albert Buckton, Peter Burns, Mr Chandler, Jack Davitt, David Farquar, Dick Flemming, Mary Fraser, John Geddes, Peter Gibson, John Gillies, Bob Hills, Eddie Jackson, Mr Kiddy, Monica Laverty, Paddy Mallen, R. Mather, Audrey Nichols, Aidan 'Nicky' Nicholson, David Picker, Bill Purdie, Mr Ridley, Malcolm Scott, Bob Seales, Jeanette Seales, Alice Thompson, Charles Thompson, Albert Tonkin, Leslie Took, Maurice Wakefield, Betty Wallace, Linda Wilson and Irene Wonders.

Special thanks to Tony Parker, Dave MacKenzie, John Jasper, Margaret MacKenzie and all at the Wallsend People's Centre who have always been available for help and advice. Paul Bream and Eric Hollerton and staff of North Tyneside Libraries. Val White for her support for the project and Durham University and Newcastle Library for supplying material. Ian S. Carr, George Nairn, John Yates and Dave Durward for additional photographs and Lisa Whiteley for proof reading.

Bibliography

David Dougan, *The History of North-East Shipbuilding*, 1968
Norman L. Middlemiss, *British Shipbuilding Yards, Volume 1: North-East Coast*, 1993
Herbert E. Taylor, *An Historical Retrospect, Swan Hunter, & Wigham Richardson, Limited*, 1932
Iris Wedgewood, *Northumberland and Durham*, 1932
A Guide To Industrial Tyneside, 1950

Newspapers and Journals

The British Shipbuilder
Evening Chronicle
The Guardian
The Journal
News Guardian
Northern Echo
The Shipyard Magazine

SHIPYARD LIFE

An aerial photograph of the Tyne showing a very different scene from today.

Swan Hunter's owes its origins to three men who were originally connected with Charles Mitchell and Co, Shipbuilders of Walker who merged with Armstrong's in 1882. Mitchell's obtained more orders for iron steamers than they could cope with and so their yard manager, John Coulson, and Richard Cooke, who was in charge of the commercial side of the company, began a separate firm of Coulson Cooke and Co at St Peter's. The site was too cramped and after they built their ninth vessel in October 1837 they moved to a 6½ acre site to the east of the yard owned by Schlesinger and Davis. By their thirteenth vessel they were in some financial difficulties and it was arranged that Charles Sheridan Swan – a brother-in-law of Charles Mitchell who had just retired as managing director of Wallsend Slipway – should take over the yard and so it became C.S. Swan and Co. Five years later, whilst returning from a trip to Russia, Mr Swan fell overboard from a cross-channel ferry and was killed by one of the paddles.

George Burton Hunter was persuaded to leave the firm of Austin and Hunter of Sunderland and, in partnership with Mrs C.S. Swan, he became the managing director of C.S. Swan Hunter on 1st January 1880. They employed 717 men and boys; the shipyard covered six and three quarter acres but it had only 270 feet of river frontage and the output for 1880 was 8,532 tons.

In January 1897 the adjoining Schlesinger and Davis yard was acquired and the public road leading to the riverside – separating the two sites – was mysteriously annexed.

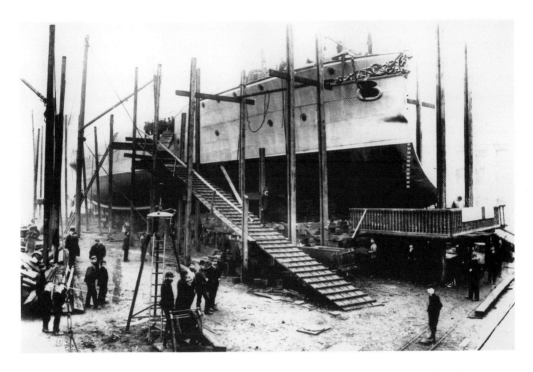

In June 1903 C.S. Swan and Hunter Ltd and Wigham Richardson and Co of the Neptune Shipyard and Engine Works became amalgamated. Then the Tyne Pontoons and Dry Docks Co at Wallsend was purchased to form the company which has, until recently dominated the town and the economy of Wallsend. This created a river frontage of some 1,400 yards with 39½ acres of works at Wallsend and a similar amount at Walker. They later acquired the firm Barclay Curles at Elderslie on Clydeside and, in 1912, opened another yard at Southwick on the Wear for the building of floating docks and caissons etc.

Clearly it was a conglomerate of some size and substance with considerable subsidiary interests in many of the supplier companies, such as Swinburnes.

They also had a passing interest in the aircraft building company Airspeed but this did not last and, after the depression of the 1930s, Swan Hunter and Wigham Richardson constrained their activities to exploiting the vast opportunities presented by the re-armament programme of a frightened Government which placed considerable orders for Naval vessels at cost-plus-ten-per-cent – and no questions asked other than delivery dates.

This was at a time when unemployment had reached over 80% at Jarrow. The unemployed of that town marched to London only to be told by the President of the Board of Trade, Walter Runciman, that the Government could do nothing and that Jarrow had to solve its own problems. Whilst the jobs emanating from the re-armament programme were thankfully received there remained a covert antipathy to the employers and the Government who had benefited from the reduction of the numbers of shipyards and virtual monopoly they had on warship production and the ordinary shipyard workers who had, over the same period, suffered only unemployment, poverty and social degradation.

That was the general atmosphere in the industry when I joined it in 1934. For most youngsters leaving school at that time meant merely to be unemployed and futureless. For those of us who had been lucky enough to get to the Grammar School there were four possible, if vague options. Outstanding soccer players might get taken on by Newcastle United – who had an option on almost every talented kid in the north. Then there was being a pupil teacher – provided that your parents had enough income to pay for your tuition. The third and fourth options were the coal mines or the shipyards. Anybody who willingly accepts a career in coal mining must be slightly mad – and a single visit to the Rising Sun Colliery convinced me of that. So that left the shipyards and with apprenticeships competitive at about 200 to one, I was very fortunate in getting one.

Bill Purdie

An extract from *A Guide to Industrial Tyneside* from 1950 describes how Swan Hunter's saw themselves at the forefront of the shipbuilding industry:

Planning Ahead

The company are pioneers in welding, which is replacing riveting to an increasing extent. The welding plants operating in this yard are of the most modern types and an X-ray apparatus for the testing of welds has been installed.

Prefabrication constitutes an advancement in ship construction and the firm has now in-hand a plan of re-organisation not only to improve the layout of the shipyards and improve cranage facilities, but also for research and pioneering to satisfy the requirements of shipowners.

In pursuance of this plan, administrative and drawing offices of modern design have been erected.

A new hydraulic riveting shed was completed in 1949 and a new 21-ton jetty crane was erected in that year. Extensions have been carried out to the jetty.

A works canteen, adjacent to the present entrance to the Wallsend shipyard, is equipped to provide an excellent mid-day meal for 1,100 to 1,200 workmen, whilst the Staff Institute provides a dining hall for the staff, together with billiards, reading and recreation rooms which offer opportunities for relaxation and social activities.

A short distance from the various departments of the company, a large recreation ground is situated, comprising association and rugby football pitches, tennis courts and bowling greens affording opportunities for physical recreation to all employees.

Apprentices to the various trades are given every encouragement, not only to become expert craftsmen but to fit themselves for the most responsible positions.

In 1940 I started at Swans as a boy labourer at fifteen. You've got to remember that a boy of fifteen wasn't as streetwise as a fifteen-year-old is today. For the first few days I was just bemused by it all. I was absolutely amazed by the noise and the amount of men who were working there. I was working in the shipwright shop with two blokes, Jimmy Ware and George Hunter. They put me on the right path and I soon got used to working there. At sixteen I started to serve my time as an electrician.

R. Mather

Swan Hunter's Middle Yard under reconstruction in 1957.

I was the third generation of my family to work in the yards – my father and grandfather had been there before me. When I was fourteen my dad said to me, 'Do you want a job at Swan Hunter's?' I said yes because at that time it was either the shipyards or the mines. I was 15 on New Year's Eve and by the 2nd January I had started work. I was just out of short trousers so it was a big shock. People used to say that when you served your National Service it made a man of you, well for me, working at Swan Hunter's certainly made me grow up fast.

Malcolm Scott

When I was fourteen we lived down the Burn at Byker and I didn't know what a shipyard was. Then we moved to Welbeck Road. Leaving school and starting in the shipyards was quite an alarming experience. When I first heard the noise of a shipyard I thought it was frightening. The noise was deafening with the riveters and caulkers all working away.

In the 1930s, conditions in Swan's were very rough. As a boy I sensed quite a lot of fear of the gaffers by the workforce. Blokes were frightened of losing their jobs. They were frightened to sneeze at the foreman in case they got the sack. Coming from school, where you were taught all about fair play, I found this attitude very strange. I also found the bad language a bit disturbing.

There was one old shipwright working in the carpenters' shop called Peter who would give you a clip around the ear if he caught you swearing. He would seize you by the boilersuit and say, 'Don't let me hear you talking like that boy, it's wicked.' He was an exception for most of the other men swore like troopers.

When I was 15 I worked as a boy labourer to the shipwrights. I worked like a little donkey. I was only lightly built and some of the stuff they gave me to carry would have made an elephant buckle at the knee.

I started serving my time when I was sixteen in the 1930s and it was a boom time as they were building ships to fight Hitler. We had a cruiser, a carrier, a battleship and destroyers to build. It was a big order of about ten ships. I was sent to work with a driller – a journeyman – to help him. I worked with him and tried to pick up the job as I was doing it. The majority of drillers I worked with used to chew baccy. They used to spit it out. I didn't even smoke so I thought it was terrible.

David Farquar

I was 13 years 10 months when I stood at the top of the bank at Swan's each morning between 7 and 7.30 with my uncle Billy Kay who was a plater's helper. He stopped the gaffers and told them I wanted a job. Well, one told me to come down and I started as a marker boy – 1127 was my number. I was 4 foot 10 inches in height and weighed 4 stone 12 pounds at the time. My first mate was Jimmy Elliot who was commonly known as Bluey Elliot because he wore blue boilersuits. He was about 25 at the time – just out of his time himself more or less – and I had to carry his bag of tools which was nearly as big as me. The first deck I went on was the destroyer called *Khartoum*. I was that frightened I felt like running off the gangway. I was dead scared when we went below to the engine room. I wished I was back at school. But I soon lost that fear.

Dick Flemming

My husband, George Wallace, worked as a plater for 50 years – from the age of fourteen (in 1925) to the age of sixty-five. For many years he worked in a cold, open-ended shed and sometimes in the open air in all weather. It was also an unhealthy workplace due to asbestos and welding fumes and there was no ear protection. Most workers had their hearing affected by the loud noises of riveters and the other things associated with heavy industry.

When my husband began work his wages were about £3 a week and with a wife and three children he often worked overtime to make ends meet. I remember one time when work was slack he had to work constant nightshift or be laid-off. However, he wasn't always so lucky and he had to find work outside the yard until the orders built up.

As I said the health and safety regulations were obviously not as good as modern day. There were often accidents. I remember on a few occasions when men fell to their deaths whilst working on the ships. I remember John Kyle of Sydney Grove, Wallsend, who fell into the deck from the side of the ship and was killed. One of the worst occasions was when a man called Ben Hogland was working in a confined space and unknown to him the oxygen bottle he was using was leaking and the oxygen had impregnated his overalls. A spark set his clothing alight and he received horrific burns. He was taken to hospital but unfortunately died.

Most family members, fathers and sons worked in the yards as it was the main source of employment. My son worked as a joiner, my brother worked as a fitter and I had four nephews who worked in the yard. Two of them played in the Swan Hunter's band. Unfortunately, one of them had to leave due to losing his hearing through working in the yards.

Whole communities lived in the shadow of the yards, with ships literally at the end of the streets. My husband's mother and her family lived within a few feet of the yards and when my children used to stay they could never sleep for the constant noise of hammering.

I had to get up early in the morning with my husband to pack his sandwiches and then I had to get my children to school before spending the day washing and cleaning overalls and work-clothes. You had to make the overalls last, as you couldn't afford to buy new ones and you didn't get them supplied. You got the boots supplied but you had to pay a weekly fee for them.

The local businesses did well. There used to be a man who stood at the top of the bank selling newspapers to the men as they entered work. Apart from Swan's, there were quite a few other yards on the Tyne who employed thousands of men. It was one of the biggest industries in the north east and most families relied on Swan's for employment. When my grandsons grow up they will be lucky if there are any yards remaining.

Betty Wallace

Our family connections with Swan Hunter's go back to the 1930s. My grandfather, Mr and Mrs Richardson, were stewards at the then named Staff Institute – the building at the very top of the bank with the clock in the garden. This building was beautifully furnished with a large kitchen, lovely dining room and facilities for table tennis, billiards, photography etc, all for use by staff members of the company. There was a lovely flat at the top of the premises where my grandparents lived. Every year they went away for a week's holiday (Race Week) and my eldest brother and sister, who were now adults, would sleep on the premises. Mother would take the rest of us down to look after the building. We had a massive garden to play in as at that time the works' canteen had not been built in the grounds. It was to us children like living in a palace. At that time the yard closed for one week's holiday per year.

My eldest brother obtained an apprenticeship to be a draughtsman. My youngest brother got an electrician apprenticeship and rose to foreman electrician. His name is Eddie Wright and when Swan's went into receivership he was paid off after forty-five years service.

My dad, Fred Wright, was day time gateman on the Main Gate. His hours were from 6 am to 5 pm. He previously worked on many ships as night watchman. He retired about 1954 when he was seventy years old.

The famous clock being re-located. Although only moving a short distance, the clock was specially cradled to protect it during lifting.

He was a good friend of 'Morris The Polis' (as everyone called him) and in Dad's latter years Morris would give him a lift to the top of the bank. At the time Morris had a Mini car and how it made it up the bank with those two onboard was a miracle. Dad, being an ex-RSM in the Army, was a big solid man.

My two sisters spent part of their working lives as tracers in Swan's. Another sister worked as a waitress in the Dry Dock Staff Canteen for managers and ships' officers, before marrying a merchant seaman.

I myself commenced work as a stock control and wages clerk in Swan's about 1950 and stayed for nine years until I left to have my first child. The new large office block had just been built then. Back in those days, all wages were paid in cash. We all took part in placing wages in packets, changing trades each week. You received the correct breakdown of cash and if we were short or had money left over, all the packets had to be re-checked. Then boxes were taken to various payout points, eg plumbers, electricians, welders etc. We younger members of staff used to swap payout stations to enable us to see the current boyfriend or hopeful future one.

The Memorial Hall was our local dance. Twice a week we would meet all the lads from Swan's. This was how I met my husband who came to work from Northern Ireland. In those days no drink was served in 'The Mem' – it was only tea etc. The doors were locked at 9.30 so the lads went for a drink first. The girls, on the other hand, would all be in the dance hall as not many frequented pubs in those days.

As you can see Swan Hunter's was a very important part of life for the Wright family. It is heartbreaking to see what happened to it, like a family friend being allowed to die.

Monica Laverty

Swan Hunter apprentice fitters in the mid 1950s.

I joined Swan Hunter's when I was 14 years of age. That might sound too young, but at the time they never brought you straight into the yard. They brought you in gradually so that you could get accustomed to the conditions and find exactly what trade suited you. So generally the boys, straight out of school at 14 and 15, were used as 'goffas'. We would go for this and go for that and make tea and go for little messages. Sometimes it was for silly little messages. The men would sometimes send you to the store for a bag of holes.

Generally, by the time you were sixteen, you had a good idea of what you wanted to be as a tradesman and you had the opportunity to pick your trade. You weren't thrown into a trade that you didn't want to do.

The trade I selected at that time was in the shipwright department. The shipwrights did most of the steelwork. Now you must remember that in those days there were no computers and work was done by very skilled tradesmen who worked in the loft – they were called loftsmen – and I started in the loft. We used to make all the templates for the construction of the boats. Nothing was done by computers. The plans used to come down from the drawing office and all the skilled, expert men used to work off the plan.

A skilled tradesman in the loft.

Later I changed my mind about my trade and I went into welding. Believe it or not, I thought there would be more money. Of course in those days there was very little time work, nearly all the trades, especially what you call the black trades, which were the caulkers, riveters, platers, shipwrights and welders, were all paid by their results – that is piece work. There used to be counters who would come round and they would count all the work you had done that week. If you didn't do a lot of work then you didn't get a lot of money.

Mr Kiddy

Shipbuilding in the 1930s was a microcosm of the class structure which existed throughout Britain. There were 32 separate trade unions and, above them, the various sub-stratum of chargehands, foremen, under-managers, and then alongside, but very separate, timekeepers, clerks and draughtsmen. The production workers had a $47^1/_2$ hour week, starting each day at 7.30 am and finishing at 5 pm with an hour for dinner (only in the deep south was it 'lunch'). We worked Monday to Friday all day plus a Saturday morning. The 'staff' of course had it easier. They started at 9 am and finished at 5 pm. This distinction was applied in the pubs as well. Foremen, having replaced their obligatory and distinctive bowler hats for cloth caps or trilby hats, invariably inhabited the 'snug' whilst the skilled and unskilled men used the bar.

Foremen wore three piece suits, skilled men wore boilersuits, engineers and fitters wore blue, and carpenters, shipwrights, platers and cranedrivers wore brown bib and brace overalls with a jacket of the same material. Joiners and cabinet makers wore the same but without the jacket. Painters, of course, and quite illogically, wore white overalls.

Bill Purdie

A bowler-hatted gaffer inspects the work.

When I started in the 1940s the head foremen were like gods. In the old days they wore bowler hats and most of them wore stiff white collars. You didn't approach them unless it was absolutely necessary. Later the foremen wore trilbies while the rank and file wore flat caps or berets.

During the Second World War electricians were brought up from the south who had not worked in shipyards before. These southern electricians were a different breed altogether. They wore trilbies which was the headgear of the foreman. They also wore suits and had their overalls in a case. So these fellas would change out of their work gear to go home. They would also wash their hands and face when they left. None of us did that and just went home wearing our work gear. We just left work dirty. You would get on a trolleybus and smell paint, tar and other shipyard smells.

R. Mather

When I first went into the yards in the 1940s you could always tell the riveters because they wore waistcoats. While the platers wore blue overalls. The managers wore white hats, the foremen wore green hats and the men were supposed to wear yellow hats. Most welders didn't bother wearing hats – anyway they got in the way of your screens.

Jack Davitt

I started when I was 14 in 1930. I had got word on the Friday to start work on the Monday at the time office at the Slipway. It was a 7.30 start which was a bit of a jump from starting school at 9 o'clock. There were eight young lads in the office – all within the pecking order. The bottom lad had a lot of running around with messages and the like. The boss used to ring his bell upstairs and the junior downstairs had to leap up and race to see what messages he wanted.

The managing director at that time was Andrew Laing. He wore a high hat and black tailed coat. Sometimes he would be out in the yard when a salesman would call to see him. So reception would ring the bell and one of the juniors came up, took the salesman's card and went off into the yard to find Mr Laing. You would be searching through the tool shop, jetty, boiler shop, copper shop, joiners, foundry and so on. You would ask people if they knew where he was and they would reply, 'Well, he was through here an hour ago.' You would get back

ages later to find he'd returned and seen the salesman. Andrew Laing knew everything that was going on – he never missed a thing. He was born in 1856 and died in 1931, so I had a year chasing him.

One of my jobs was to sort the pay tins. You used to get your wages in a pay tin. Your work's number was painted on the top and your wages was put inside with a ticket. You had to hand in your time card and you got your pay tin in exchange. On Saturday morning our job, as time office boys, was to get these tins out of a big box they had been thrown in and sort them into work's number again. You were sometimes lucky to find some money inside which had been overlooked.

As a boy I was paid 7/6 for a 50 hour week. That's not very much. I had to keep a rabbit out of my sixpence pocket money. So that left very little for courting.

Albert Buckton

In the 1950s I started working at Swan Hunter's as a draughtsman. The drawing office was down the yard, strategically placed in a wooden building under which the steam trains ran. Every time a train went past the steam came up through the floor.

Hugh Archibold

The Tynemouth to Newcastle train passes the entrance to Swan's a few days before the service was withdrawn in July 1973.

Vickers-Armstrongs Limited

NAVAL YARD, WALKER, NEWCASTLE UPON TYNE, 6.

Certificate of Apprenticeship.

We, Vickers-Armstrongs Ltd., hereby certify that *J 105*

Allan Blackett has served as an Apprentice

Joiner with this Company for the full period of five

years from *1 . 2 . 40* to *2 . 3 . 45* and has

satisfactorily completed this apprenticeship.

We further certify that *Allan Blackett*

has observed the rules and conditions of employment during the full

period of his apprenticeship.

For VICKERS-ARMSTRONGS LTD.,

Date *29 . 3 . 45*

J. M. Amslin. ....Director.

A certificate of Apprenticeship.

When I turned up for work on my first day I was sent home. I had finished school at 14 and assumed I would start work at the end of the shipyard fortnight's holiday. I reported for work about the 7th August even though my fifteenth birthday wasn't until the 14th. So when I went in I was told, 'You can't start yet you're not fifteen.' I started on the 17th August and worked a year as an office boy. I started on the shop floor when I was 16. I went to training school for six months to give me the basics and then after that I went from department to department. Then when I was 20 I was put on the boats working with journeymen.

I used to work for the Wallsend Slipway which ran a department called the FOD. It was the fitting-out department at Swan's but I was paid by the Slipway. I used to start at 8 o'clock and finished at 4 o'clock but was paid from 7.30 to 4.30 – we got half an hour's travelling time.

Bob Seales

My first wage when I was fourteen was ten shillings a week. I used to give my mam seven and six to keep me and I would be left with half a crown. So with two and six I used to go to the pictures and smoke.

Mr Ridley

An Apprentice Indenture dated 9th October 1936. Included in the conditions were:

That during the term of his apprenticeship he shall regularly attend Educational Evening Classes approved of by the Company, and pay the fees for the same, it being agreed, however, that the Apprentice shall not be required to pay more than five shillings in fees per session, the Company paying the remainder (if any).

The Company shall pay the Apprentice the following wages when at work:-

When Employed on Time Work

For the First year at the rate of 5/ per week of normal hours.

"	Second	"	6/	"
"	Third	"	8/	"
"	Fourth	"	10/	"
"	Fifth	"	12/	"

The parent shall be answerable for the due performance of this contract by the Apprentice, and the Parent so agrees. The Parent also agrees that during the period of apprenticeship he will provide the Apprentice with all proper and necessary food and wearing apparel, and with all such things as the Company might otherwise under liability to provide for him.

When I first started going out with Bob (my husband) I was earning more money than he was. He was serving his time and his wages were very poor. A lot of his pals who were working elsewhere earned more than he did. But it was worth it for the lads who slogged away for the five years of their apprenticeship. Once he was out of his time his wages just snowballed and he was guaranteed a job.

Jeanette Seales

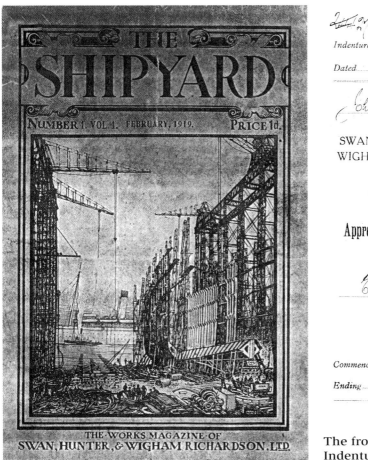

The first *Shipyard Magazine* from 1919.

Indenture No. *1080*

Dated *9ᵗ October* 19*36*

John Marshall

AND

SWAN. HUNTER, AND WIGHAM RICHARDSON
LIMITED.

Apprenticeship Indenture

AS

Electrician

Commencing *16ᵗ February 1935.*

Ending *5ᵗ March, 1940*

The front of an Apprentice Indenture.

In February 1919 the *Shipyard Magazine* was launched for workers of Swan, Hunter & Wigham Richardson Ltd. Priced at 1d it was 'thought that a Works Magazine might play a very useful part by bringing together the many interests in different yards and works controlled by the firm on the Tyne and Wear.' The first issue included this article by G.B. Hunter:

The 'Hours' Question

I cordially welcome the first number of the *Shipyard Magazine*. I hope it will be not only a source of much pleasure to all those who read it and a channel of interesting communication between the members of staff and other workers in the associated works, but will also be the means of promoting goodwill and a friendly mutual understanding and co-operation between all classes of employers and employed. I hope the Editor will open its columns to, and will so far as space allows, specially welcome contributors from wage-earners – men, women and apprentices – as well as from foreman and other members of the staff. I think there is no reason why it should not be many sided and represent many views.

A letter signed 'One of your workmen' has been addressed to me as

the Chairman of Messrs Swan, Hunter & Wigham Richardson, Limited, in which a temperate appeal is made for the adoption of a 44-hour week, and in which the writer says, 'If you sir, being the head of one of the largest shipbuilding firms in the world could be the means of getting this concession for the men you would earn the gratitude of thousands of men.' The writer of the letter does not think a stoppage for breakfast desirable, as he says 'a half-hour for breakfast would mean more than half an hour before they really settled down to work.'

Well, any temperate and reasonable request always appeals strongly to me and I would always respond to it if I could – but is this request reasonable? I fear it would be very selfish and unreasonable as well as very short-sighted, if for the sake of a temporary popularity our Company were to argue to a big innovation which might be a very dangerous experiment. If followed by other trades, and unless all workers would do as much in 44 hours as in 54, it would materially tend to keep up the high cost of living and would reduce 'real wages' and be injurious to the interests of all wage-earners as well as employers. That is, I believe, not a matter of opinion, but a certainty. We cannot have the goods unless we produce them, and we cannot buy cheaply the things we need unless we produce them cheaply. The

This postcard – captured during dinner at Swan's – was posted 25th April 1927.

workers have always in the past greatly benefited by increased production, and no employers, nor capitalists, nor anything else can prevent them from benefiting by it in the future.

It would handicap British manufacturing and British workers in getting a fair share of the world's business; and in the long run it might result, and in fact it would result, in lower 'real wages' and in unemployment on account of the contracts from buyers of ships and our other products going to Japan, China, Germany, Holland and America, instead of coming to England, Scotland, Wales and Ireland. Let us not deceive ourselves. In most of these countries in normal times ships can already be built at lower costs than in British yards. Where the cost is low the orders will go …

I wish I could believe that at present a reduction of hours below 47 hours would be safe or wise.

I wish we could avoid all disputes! One thing we can do in regard to the hours question. We can provide more and better canteen accommodation.

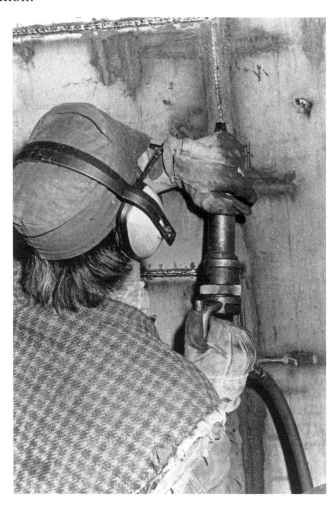

I started at Swan Hunter's in the 1940s when you had to be in at 7.30 am. I lived in Laburnum Avenue, Wallsend at that time. There were times, when the buzzer was blown at 25 minutes past 7, I would be just getting on my bike at home. But, there wasn't many days when I was late for work.

My first job in the yards was working for a foreman plater. His office was in the fabrication shed. My first job was at 7.30 to light an old cast-iron stove in the office. I would use scrap wood which I would find around the yard, usually from broken up templates. The coke which I used was the same coke that they used to heat the rivets. When I was 14 I think my wage was about 14/6 a week.

Then I went from working in the shipyard to being an office boy in the drawing office. I think I went up to about 15 shillings a week. The drawing office was built over the main railway and you would have steam trains coming through. There were short walks between the various drawing offices – there was an electric office, a steel office, a design office. To walk between them there was a cat walk of wooden planks. So if there was a locomotive coming you had to get off this cat walk very quickly. If you didn't you would be likely to be covered in steam. The cat walks were made of wood and were very slippy in the wet so it was easy to slip when you heard the trains coming. It was even harder if you had an armful of plans.

Albert Tonkin

When I joined Swan's I went into the Drawing Office School. We went in absolutely raw. The first things we were taught was how to sharpen a pencil, how to load a drawing pen and how to chalk and stretch new linen. We also had to learn how to print with an old school nib on cloth, because a plan has to be legible. It doesn't matter nowadays because computers have made many of our old skills unnecessary. I had joined the company to draw ships using my brain and eye and hand co-ordination – not using a computer.

When I started you had to provide your own equipment. I can't remember getting any allowance from the firm to buy it. Some trades got an allowance for their equipment. We got a 'draughtsman's box' which cost 10 shillings. My first wage was only 27/6 a week so 10 shillings was a lot. We were allowed to pay 1 shilling a week for 10 weeks. The boxes were about a yard long and there were trays to keep our equipment in. We kept our slide rules in there too – this was before calculators. We used slide rules and log books for all our calculation. Kids these days don't know what log tables are – they don't need to. I hated it when computers came in. I'm very computer unfriendly. I was always scared stiff of wiping everything out.

Eddie Jackson

I came up from London in 1941 to work in the yards and the contrast was amazing. Up here I found the friendliness beautiful – people would share their tea or bait with you. In London it was every man for themselves. Up here everyone seems to know each other. I was twenty when I started and I was soon called up to serve in the war. I was glad really. After the war you were entitled to claim your job back which I did. At this time everyone was on piece work. I think it was the start of the downfall of the shipyards when they did away with it. When men were on piece work they would work right up to the buzzer. You could still see welder's flashers when the buzzer was going. But once we went on to time work everyone worked at the same speed and knocked off together.

Charles Thompson

I started work on the 24th June 1946. I had been serving in the Navy and was at home from leave just prior to being demobbed when I inadvertently got a job. My brother had written to Swan's and asked if there was a vacancy in the apprentice school. They told him if he'd had a matriculation they would have started him. So I went down and saw the technical manager, explained that I had this and he said I could start on the understanding that I would do a six-year naval architecture course from 1946 to '52. So I was taken-on on the 24th June and that date was inscribed on my stool. Everybody had their own personal stool.

When I started we worked 44 hours a week. In the office we were working a five and a half day week – we knocked off at one o'clock on a Saturday afternoon. Then the hours were reduced to 43, 42, 40 and then eventually it came down to 37$^{1}/_{2}$ hours. In 1946 one of our jobs was to keep a note of the number of various trades which were employed in the yard. At that time there were between twelve and thirteen thousand at Wallsend. Then when we amalgamated with Readhead's and Hebburn, Walker and Haverton Hill the total manpower was something of the order of around thirty thousand. Since then, slowly but surely, it has been whittled away. Of course modernisation and new machinery coming into the yards greatly effected a labour-intensive industry. I can recall in the design office the way calculations were done on large foolscap sheets which were then passed on to a second person to check. We used to have a calculating machine which was about two feet long by about four feet. Then, later on, I was in charge of the design department and I was shown a

Harry Miller demonstrates the finer points of shipbuilding to a group of Swan's apprentices at the Newcastle College of Arts and Technology in the late 1970s.

calculator the size of a typewriter. They were £150 each and we bought two. But of course when you bought things like this you had to start looking around at the manpower they could save.

Leslie Took

I started my apprenticeship as a welder in 1966. My first impression of a shipyard was the noise. I think I was probably frightened at the time because you were hit by this wall of noise and it just went on and on and on. At that time they didn't issue ear defenders.

There were initiations for young lads new to the yards. They would tie you up to posts or put squeegee soap into your pockets or old chips into your sandwich box.

Tony Parker

When I first started I was sent to the welding school by Swan's Dry Dock. You taught yourself, really – by trial and error. Eventually, when you went on the ship, they'd give you a simple job at first, then a more difficult one as you got the knack of it.

Jack Davitt

The first ship I worked on was a super tanker called the *Tyne Pride*.
The ship was absolutely huge. It was about 80 to 90 foot deep from the
main deck into the tanks – you could stand three houses on top of each
other in there. I was an apprentice and found looking down into the
tanks really daunting – in fact frightening. One day I was working with
another apprentice and we had to sound the tanks. To do that, you had
a tape with a brass weight on the end and you dropped it to the bottom
of the tank. I said to the other lad, 'I'll go to the bottom of the tank and
you go to the top.' So I climbed all the way down while he climbed all
the way up. When I got to the bottom I stood and waited and waited. I
then shouted up to him but heard nothing. I finally decided to climb all
the way up to look for him. It was about a five to ten minute climb.
The ship was still being built and the outer shell on the top unit was
missing. I found the lad standing on a beam which was about two foot
wide and he was clinging to the bulk head with his fingernails literally
stuck in the metal. It was now I realised he was terrified of heights.
There was no way I could move him so I went to get someone from the
medical centre. We got a crane with a skip to lift him – or wedge him –
from the bulk head. He eventually pulled himself together and I had to
get somebody else to do the job. He was an apprentice who learnt a
good lesson that day.

Mr Chandler

When I was twenty-one, and after serving my apprenticeship at JL Thompson's shipyard on the Wear, I left my employment there to seek a fresh challenge and to gain more experience in other yards. In April I began work as a shipwright at Swan Hunter's Wallsend shipyard and although I worked there for only four months, the experience was so interesting that I can vividly remember my time at the yard.

After showing my union card to the two shop stewards to prove that I was 'in benefit' I was sent to work with a shipwright called Ted who was a man in his fifties. Ted was a canny bloke who sort of took me under his wing, and on Fridays we used to go for a couple of pints during the dinner hour.

We worked on the *Windsor Lion* – a 240,000 ton oil tanker. I had thought that the ships at Thompson's were big at 150,000 tons but the size of this oil tanker was phenomenal. I can remember the plate was so heavy that hydraulic jacks had to be used to fair-up almost everything. As construction progressed, huge heavy duty nets were strewn across the centre tanks to prevent certain death for some unfortunate worker who fell from deck head staging. I must admit that the safety nets gave me much more confidence when working at those great heights. When I worked on the Wear safety nets weren't used.

There were other new experiences for me, like the novelty of using a wooden hand screen for tack welding, which was made in the yard. The normal 'bought in' manufactured issue was restricted to head screens. Another oddity which was indigenous to Tyneside yards was that some men addressed others, whose name they didn't know, by 'Hammer' instead of using 'mate' which I was accustomed to. There was also the fascination of Hadrian's Wall which ended in the shipyard, and Ted showed me a plaque attached to a wall below the gaffer's office at the top of the berth which said the stones were from the Roman Wall.

There were the characters, of course – every shipyard had them. But one who stands out in my memory is 'Clogger', so called because he wore wooden clogs for work, the likes of which I hadn't seen before – or since.

There was plenty of work on the Tyne then and there was a shortage of skilled labour, unlike Wearside yards where it was fairly difficult to find work. Dilution had been accepted by the Boilermakers Union branches on the Tyne and at Wallsend I sometimes heard odd ones being referred to as 'the dilutee'. To the uninitiated, a dilutee was a man who hadn't served a recognised apprenticeship but was trained in a trade later in his working life. There was a resentful attitude towards a dilutee. It was as if he was a second class citizen or he had done something criminal. 'They're only any good for tacking,' was a comment made to me which oozed with bitter resentment. I hadn't come across a dilutee shipwright before, and I didn't have a problem with them. I got the impression that they were resented even more than Mackems, and the remark made to wind me up: 'Ya tyekin tha breed outa wor mooths,' was probably directed towards a dilutee more seriously.

Shortly after I started at Swan's I was approached on different occasions by three disgruntled boilermakers who were keen to tell me of their bitter experiences on Wearside. A burner said he had lost his job at Thompson's after a launch because the shop steward insisted that management first pay off Tynesiders before Wearside men. And there was a shipwright who had been offered a job at Thompson's but the shop stewards wouldn't let management start him because he was in a Tyneside union branch. Another shipwright – a shop steward – exclaimed: 'Sunderland! They paid me off through there when I was a boy!' As if it was in some way my fault. Judging by his appearance it was probably something which happened to him before I was born.

However, May 1974 could have been a good time for a Sunderland lad working on the Tyne. Sunderland were the FA Cup holders and Newcastle in their attempt to in some way emulate that great achievement were beaten by Liverpool three goals to nil. After enjoying the game on TV I decided that a tact of quiet smugness would be wise in a yard where Sunderland supporters were a rarity.

I enjoyed my short experience at the Wallsend yard and I can honestly say that I was treated fairly there. I often wondered what happened to Ted.

Peter Gibson

The *Evening Chronicle* of 9th September 1977 reported the start and end of four careers at Swan Hunter's Neptune Yard:

They're all hard timers

Hard times can bridge any generation gap, as the lads at British Shipbuilders, in Wallsend, know well.

Although jobs have been given to teenagers at the Neptune Yard two old men will soon be out of work.

But 76-year-old messenger Tommy Cook and his mate Joe Summers, aged 75, bear no grudges.

They see the scheme worked out between the unions and the management in an attempt to cut the dole queue among school-leavers as a good one and they are making way for the youngsters without bitterness.

Tommy said: 'I was in and out of a job during the depression. I know what it is like. I worked as a joiner and then started as a messenger in 1968 when other blokes of my age were retiring. It's a good job and one which the lads will enjoy. I'll miss all my mates in the yards because I know everyone so well, but I'm going to have a rest now.'

Joe Summers came to the yard five years ago to begin work as a messenger after a life down the pits. He leaves at the end of this month and Mr Clark goes in October.

Youngsters Mick Viney, of Richmond Road, South Shields, and Malcolm Charlton of Mill Lane, Hebburn both 17, are the lucky ones.

Both faced the daunting prospect of life on the dole when the opportunity of working in the yards was presented to them.

Mick said: 'I was at the end of a work experience programme and I didn't think there was any chance of getting a job.'

Like Mick, Malcolm left school with six CSE passes, but he said: 'They are no good. Employers always ask for O-levels. Now we can train to be painters or slingers because we take up jobs in the yards when we are 18 and new lads will start as messengers.'

I left school when I was 14 and worked as a milk roundsman. Then one day I dropped 2 or 3 bottles of milk and I was too scared to go back – so that was the end of that. Then I was a painter and decorator. I was going to serve my time as a painter and decorator, but then the war broke out. I was still too young to join up so I went into the shipyards. It was 1940 and I was 16. It was either the shipyards or the mines. So I went for the lesser of two evils.

Some of the men would tease the kids who were very vulnerable. There was a lot of it which went on. They used to send you for a long stand and things like that. When I first started they tried to send me for some rubber nails, and another time for a rubber hammer. But I never fell for it – I was a bit too fly for that.

I started to serve my time when I was 16 and I went into the Navy when I was 18. I served in the Navy until the end of the war. I then came back. I was on what was known as the 'interrupted apprenticeship scheme' and I finished my apprenticeship when I was 22. I was a welder until I took early retirement when I was 62. I was glad to leave. The shipyards were a terrible place to be. Then conditions were awful – some places were like nightmares.

Jack Davitt

Autobiography
by Ripyard Cuddling

My cap too big, my bait too small
I stood beside the shipyard wall
The buzzer ringing in my ears
I remember I was close to tears.

My school books had been put away
For this was my first working day
And I was at a tender age
A question mark on life's first page.

I saw the workmen hurry past
And felt my courage melting fast
Bewildered in a strange terrain
I looked for sympathy in vain.

With eager eyes I searched each face
Each runner in that morning race
But they had troubles of their own
And I was left to stand alone.

But youth will always have its way
And somehow I survived that day
And that was how it all began
That morning I became a man.

Apprenticed to the welding trade
I struggled hard to make the grade
The squarest peg, the roundest hole
The choice was this or digging coal.

I often think on looking back
That somewhere I went off the track
The road I took was wrong somehow
I've plenty time to rue it now.

For forty years my cheeks were wet
With shipyard tears and shipyard sweat
I've hurried to the buzzer's call
And toiled on vessels large and small.

I often wonder, can it be?
That boy so long ago was me?
That boy so innocent and green
The 'Never was' who might have been.

As I recall those distant years
And see myself so close to tears
My cap was not too big at all
It was my head that was too small.

Shipyard scenes from the 1990s

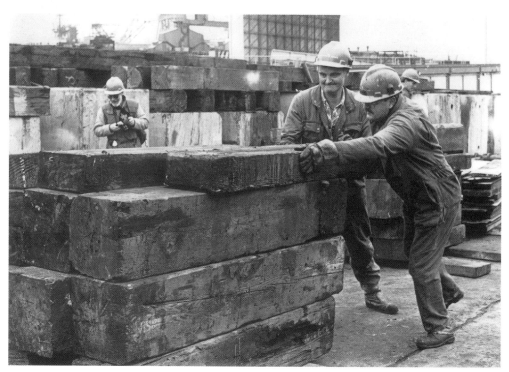

SECTION TWO

THE SHIPS

The *Esso Northumbria* which was launched in May 1969 and left the river the following year. Crowds flocked to the banks of the Tyne to see this huge supertanker.

There is something indescribable in the sight of a launch, something that is both pleasure and pain. Expressions grow tense and strained, men hold there breath, builders, owners, engineers responsible for dredging, are all taut with anxiety ... Like some noble water-bird she glides slowly forward, and as she slips serenely into that element which is now to be her home, beset with that fear of disaster we watch her. Alone in all the world her safety matters, nothing else is of any account. With relief we see the little tugs waiting, minute and fussy – they are ready for her. Her beautiful body is yet a helpless thing, without power of its own. Her engines, her lifeblood, have still to be given to her. A flood tide of exquisite relief sweeps over the watchers, she is in the river, she is swinging round, she is alongside the bank, she lies below us, mute and glorious. She is launched.

Iris Wedgwood
Northumberland and Durham (1932)

The 1950 *A Guide to Industrial Tyneside* described Swan Hunter's proud record:

From the incorporation of the company in 1903 to the end of 1950 the output of the Wallsend and Neptune shipyards in gross tonnage

The launch of the *Athelking* from Swan's.

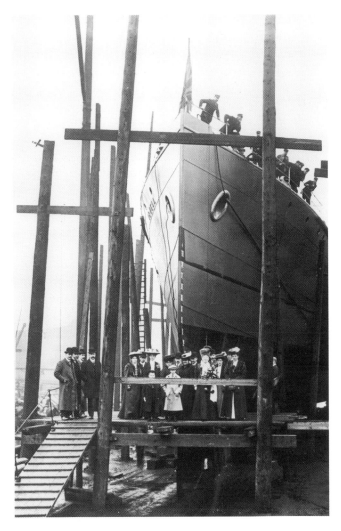

reached the figure of nearly 4 million tons, and headed the world's list of annual shipbuilding tonnage on no less than eight occasions. The last appearance at the head of the list was in 1930, when it created a world's record by launching 37 ships of a total tonnage of 213,229.

We were working on the aircraft carrier *Illustrious* when the Falklands War started. It was nearing completion and we had to speed up so it would be ready to go to the South Atlantic. I think we were working seven days a week and twelve hour shifts so they were long, long days. I had a lump in my throat the day we launched the ship because it was like losing a part of you. We had become very attached to the ship and we were very proud of it. It almost became like a home to us as we spent so long on board.

Then we built its sister ship the *Ark Royal* which was another one that I worked on from the beginning to the end. Because of the

Ark Royal's status, and the history that famous name has, I had an even bigger lump in my throat when that one went away. It was a ship where everybody seemed to muck in together no matter what problems we had. A lot of men were really proud to be part of that ship.

As the ships were being finished off you could take your family on board to have a look around. I took my dad to see the *Ark Royal*. He had worked in the yards for over 30 years – mostly as a driller – but had been out of the yards for a few years through ill health. When I took him on to the *Ark Royal* I had placed a drilling machine at the top of the gangway and when he saw it he had tears in his eyes. His memories came flooding back when we went round the ship. He really missed working in the yards.

Mr Chandler

A young lady from the offices was normally selected to present a bouquet to the person who launched the ship. At one launch a girl from our office was selected. She was a bit of a 'glamour queen' and wore the most fantastic dress you have ever seen. It was a real flouncy dress and as she walked up the steps to present the bouquet you could see her suspenders. All the lads in the yard loved this and were cheering. She got a bigger cheer than the 'important lady' who had come to launch the ship. When she got back to the office our boss tore strips off her.

Charles Thompson

We had great fun at launches. Everyone was given permission to go to each launch if we wanted and of course we young girls never missed one. Our boss used to say, 'I don't know why you want to go to everyone – they are all the same.' He had obviously forgotten about being young.

Monica Laverty

I can remember when the *Northumbria* was launched – it was two hundred and fifty thousand tons. I was standing at Cullercoats when it left the Tyne and was so impressed by its size – it absolutely dwarfed the North Pier. Even though I had seen it being built in the yard and saw how it dwarfed all the buildings around it – I was still impressed.

Leslie Took

There was one ship that was launched with a coconut rather than a bottle of champagne. It was an Indian ship which was designed to take pilgrims to India.

Maurice Wakefield

The launch of HMS *York* from Swan Hunter's, June 1982.

The launch of the *Esso Hibernia* in 1971.

The *Esso Hibernia* being manoeuvred by tugs after launch.

Sea trials were happy times. You could have all sorts of adventures out in the North Sea. I was once on a guided missile destroyer which was travelling very fast – let's say 25-30 miles an hour rather than knots. They were about 4,000 tons with two gas turbines with a combined 50,000 horse power. So we're going along and I look over the side of the ship and see a dolphin – it was beautiful. The ship's chugging along with the dolphin swimming alongside with just a flick of its tail. Then suddenly he flicks his tail a little bit harder and he shoots ahead of us – and he didn't have a gas turbine on board.

Another time when we were on sea trials, I was standing on the bridge and there was some cormorants flying alongside us. It looked like one of them was tiring and we could see he was lagging behind the others. We thought he was going to give up then all of a sudden he took one deep breath and he was away.

One time we were on a ship when it was a lovely clear day. I looked out the bilge window and there was an aeroplane alongside and the pilot waved at us.

When you are out at sea the same thing would always happen when the work was finished – out came all the fishermen and over went the lines. Everybody would be fishing and what they caught was put into a bag with their name on it and popped into the freezer to take home.

Hugh Archibold

Launch Days

Mauretania

S.S. MAURETANIA LAUNCHED AT WALLSEND SEP. 20th 1906. THE LARGEST SHIP AFLOAT. T.A.G.

LAUNCH OF THE S.S. MAURETANIA (THE LARGEST SHIP IN THE WORLD) SEPT. 20 1906.

Driving through the *Mauretania's* funnel.

You got good money for going on the sea trials. When you first went on the trials it was like an adventure but by the end of the trip it was sheer boredom. You are out for a week; you can't go anywhere and if the weather was bad you couldn't even go on deck in case you got washed over the side. Once you had finished your work you had hours with nothing to do.

There was a time, however, when we were working on some tankers which went out to Germany and into a dry dock. Then we went on what was called 'day work'. You worked like you would in the yard – 7.30 to 4.30 – and then you went ashore every night which was brilliant. We would then come back and kip on the ship. Other times, when we were abroad, if you worked through for say twelve hours the gaffer might say, 'Hey you've done a canny job – knock-off tomorrow dinnertime and I'll see you the following morning.' That was great. If we were working in Holland we would be straight off to Amsterdam. One time we went to Portugal and we were given a half-day off for doing a long job. Four of us went off to the beach. We were lying there in the sun and getting paid for it. It was brilliant. Mind this didn't happen very often.

Aidan Nicholson

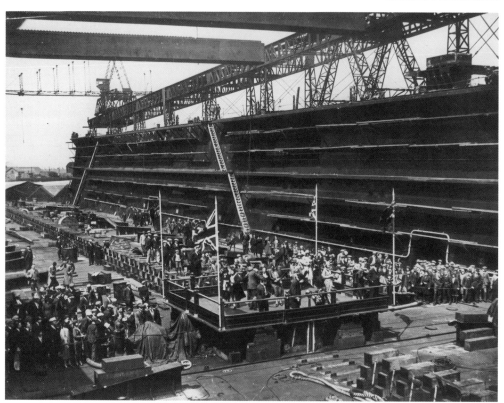

The Singapore Dock – the largest floating dock in the world – leaves Wallsend in 1928.

The Legend of the Million Ton Tanker
by Ripyard Cuddling

A group of yards along the Tyne
Decided they would all combine
To pool their skills and then, perhaps,
United they would beat the Japs.

The early spring of 'Sixty Eight'
Saw all these brains behind one gate,
By August their endeavour won
A tanker of a million ton.

This order set the Tyne alight,
The future now at last looked bright,
And so they booked the City Hall
To hold a celebration ball.

The ball was quite a grand affair
And everyone of note was there
And members of the working class
Rubbed shoulders with the upper brass.

A merry night was had by all
At Swan's amalgamation ball
But all good things must end it's true
And there was still a job to do.

Production soon got under way
And the keel was down by Guy Fawkes'
Day;
A mighty keel of six inch plate,
It stretched from Swan's to Walkergate.

The longy butts were ten feet high,
They made the strongest caulkers cry
And platers laboured in the sheds
With tie plates big as wing bulkheads.

The stagers all wore parachutes
And rubber suckers on their boots;
One counter name of Bobby Corbett
Fell off the mast – he's still in orbit.

The journey to the after peak
On foot took half a working week.
And, though the workers had to hike,
Each gaffer had a motor bike.

The centre tanks were such a height
The upper deck was out of sight.
And, up among the beams and struts,
Two helicopters checked the butts.

Inside the bulbous bow one day
Two foremen welders lost their way;
Alas! these two intrepid men
Were never seen again.

The human mind could scarcely grip
The magnitude of this great ship;
This miracle of Tyneside skill
Was, for the Japs, a bitter pill.

It wasn't just the Japanese
That Swan Hunter failed to please;
Before the launching celebrations
The town would need some alterations.

The council sat in grim debate
And hammered out the township's fate.
They talked all day of sweat and toil
That night they burned the midnight oil.

Upon the map they drew a mark
From Carville Road to Wallsend Park;
The drag chains for the giant ship
Would run right through this fated strip.

The Mayor arose and sad of voice
Said, 'Gentlemen, we have no choice,
Although we love our dear old town,
We'll have to pull half of it down.

The 'Mem' and the Masonic Hall
And Woolworth's too will have to fall,
The 'Ship' the 'Penny Wet' as well
And even Simpson's Grand Hotel.'

The morning sky the sun was greeting
When Wallsend council left their
meeting
And civic heads were bowed with cares,
And civic cheeks were wet with tears.

But hope forever springs eternal
For there in that same morning's
'Journal'
Was news that gladdened every eye,
In the next verse I will tell you why …

The news on pages one and two
Came like a blot out of the blue –
The ship built by great combine
Was two feet wider than the Tyne.

The council all began to sing,
The Mayor danced a highland fling,
And passers-by turned round to stare
At civic duts tossed in the air.

The council's cup of joy was full
But elsewhere hopes were rather dull;
The heads of Swan Hunter's group
Were well and truly in the soup.

The brains assembled in their lair,
Sir John himself was in the chair –
'The problem gentlemen (I quote)
Is how to get our ship afloat.'

They sat all day and made their plans
And ended with a show of hands;
Their scheme, though born of
desperation,
Resolved a tricky situation.

On Monday, June the twenty third,
The most amazing launch occurred,
They turned the berth the other way
And launched the ship at Whitley Bay.

It thundered past the 'Rising Sun'
This monster of a million ton,
High Farm Estate and Bigges Main
Will never be the same again.

No architect could ever cure
The damage done to Shiremoor
And all agreed it was a pity
The drag chains wrecked the Spanish
City.

The backwash when it hit the sea
Drowned fifty pigs at Peterlee,

The BBC reported panic
When monster crabs invaded Alnwick.

At last the giant super tanker
In sixty fathoms lay at anchor,
A massive structure painted grey
It brooded over Whitley Bay.

Three shifts of fitters toiled like slaves
As this great monster rode the waves,
Completing in one busy year
The engine and the steering gear.

The happy day arrived at last
When, pennants flying from her mast,
The giant ship got under way
And left the shores of Whitley Bay.

But trouble seemed to dog this ship
For, early on her maiden trip,
She turned to starboard off Penzance
And dislocated half of France.

De Gaulle, who seemed a trifle vexed,
To Wilson said, 'Whatever next?
Your ship has caused grave
complications
I'm off to tell United Nations.'

A block vote by the 'Iron Curtain'
And the tanker's fate was sealed for
certain,
In spite of Harold Wilson's pleas
They banned her from the Seven Seas.

Mid scenes of grief and deep emotion
They towed her to the Arctic Ocean
And there in that far Northern clime
She's doing penance for her crime.

Though politicians fought her case,
They couldn't save the tanker's face.
In spite of all their flowery words,
She's now a sanctuary for birds.

Out there, beneath the Arctic skies,
A part of France's coast-line lies
And traces too, you can be sure,
Of Bigges Main and Shiremoor.

WORKING
CONDITIONS

Nightshift at Swan's.

Building 'ships to perfection' is not easy. It requires a wide range of scientific knowledge allied to tough physical resources. For ships today are highly complicated vessels, often replete with scientific equipment. Yet they are still built – and probably always will be – by sheer, demanding, hard work. A shipyard is no place for a weakling. On the contrary, the open-air life, especially in winter, the huge, draughty sheds and the ringing racket of the drills and welding machinery provide a good test of anyone's mettle.

David Dougan
The History of North East Shipbuilding (1968)

I think you had to have a sense of humour to work in the shipyards because you were working under really bad conditions. In winter it was awful. You'd get a horrible wind coming off the Tyne and you would be freezing to death. And the stories of gaffers kicking the fires out are all true. I can't describe how bad the conditions were. I became a safety rep so I could actually do something about it.

Tony Parker

The conditions were terrible in the yards but camaraderie was great. You had to have a sense of humour to survive – like in the trenches in the First World War. In any shipyard you weren't allowed to have fires to keep you warm. But one particular winter we had some machines – they were electronic things driven by pneumatics – which wouldn't operate in the cold and so they had these big braziers keeping the machines warm while we were freezing. That incident showed that in a shipyard, machines were more important than men.

Some of the managers were good – some were bad. There were a lot of tyrants. There was also a lot of class distinction in the shipyards. Some of the managers were so conceited they wouldn't even speak to you. How do you manage anybody without speaking to them. It was pathetic. I also knew foremen like that. Give them a green hat and they were much too important to speak to you.

Jack Davitt

Safety measures at Swan Hunter's improved dramatically in recent years. Thirty years ago men were walking around with their own shoes or overalls. There were no safety hats then. Accidents were common with men getting metal in their eyes, or spanners, nuts and bolts falling on your head, or tripping over or falling down. Men would fall off ladders, down manholes which were covered up or from staging that didn't have handrails. It was terrible. A lot of these types of accidents could have been prevented very easily.

Then things started to change and tougher safety measures came in with people starting to be better educated. However, you can't just force people to change – you need to educate and coax them. Workers started to then wear proper overalls, safety boots with steel caps on them, gloves and goggles. It was just simple measures but the number of accidents quickly fell.

Mr Chandler

In the 1930s workmen didn't have lockers for their clothes and so if it happened to rain on the way to work, or during the day, they just had to work in those damp clothes all day. Washing facilities just did not exist. There were a few taps around but they were outside and not placed or available for washing. Some of us apprentices used to acquire tins of soft soap that was applied to the ways when a ship was about to be launched and we used to wash the filth off our hands before we went home – provided there wasn't a foreman near the tap.

Toilet facilities were unbelievably primitive. There were two long troughs down each side of a shed about five feet or so apart. There was a plank seat on the inner facing side of narrow partitions which merely separated the sitters but allowed them no privacy whatsoever. They could talk to each other and pass the *Daily Mirror* up and down the line if there was any spicy story in it – and of course newspaper had other more functional capabilities when torn into quarter pages.

To use these 'facilities' it was necessary to surrender your time card, and your entry and exit times were recorded by a man in a small booth. Three minutes each day was the allocation and a fine imposed for each minute in excess of the allowance. So there was a considerable financial sanction on those who had over-imbibed on a Sunday night and suffered the inevitable consequence on a Monday. Upon entering this salubrious unsanitary sanctuary one was given three small sheets of toilet paper – called by the clients 'a scraper, a wiper and a polisher' – and so the addition of a sheet of newspaper was always a bonus.

Large cisterns at the end of the troughs flushed water automatically about every ten minutes or so. When they operated, a huge tidal wave shot down the length of the trough collecting on its way all that deposited therein. The cisterns announced their activity – but not too

SWAN HUNTERS SHIPYARD WALLSEND FROM HEBBURN

loudly and remember many of the workmen had industrial deafness –
and while the more agile customers rose quickly from their section of
the planks the less agile got a kind of involuntary bidet experience
which, being cold water, came as quite a fundamental shock. It was
truly amazing the height that could be achieved by a middle-aged man
from a sitting position with his trousers around his ankles when that
tidal wave approached.

One of the toilets was at the riverside and raised about six feet above
the ground. The inboard side was punched with holes in a sort of
cornucopia pattern which disguised its function from visitors but
allowed hundreds of freezing draughts to add to the discomforts of the
squatting clients.

Those working on the ships which were being constructed on the
stocks had a problem if they wanted to go to the lavatory. They had to
climb to the upper deck, then descend the gangway to ground level and
cross the shipyard to the lavatory so the urgent and the lazy didn't
bother. Others, like me, would rather have died than use those toilets.

The offices, of course, had flush toilets and proper washbasins and
towels although their need to clean themselves was considerably less
than those in the actual shipyard – but that was part of the illogical and
pure class separation within the personnel of the shipyards.

Bill Purdie

The toilets were just troughs and some places were just planks over the river.

Bob Hills

For a young boy, straight out of school, going to the toilets could be daunting. The new toilets were alright but the old ones were in such a state. There was sometimes a queue of twenty or thirty fellas. An old man would cut up newspaper and give you two sheets. If you took too long – perhaps reading the paper or having a smoke – he would go up with a wet mop to get you out. There was no locks on the doors because as soon as you put a lock on somebody would take it off and steal it. So I would be there with my three foot rule pressed against the door to stop anyone coming in.

Malcolm Scott

In the 1930s/40s I worked in a joiners' store which we called the ice house because it was so cold. We would leave our brushes in a pot of water overnight and when we came in the following morning it would be frozen. We had to break the ice to get our brushes out. Talk about Dickensian conditions.

Bob Hills

Years ago they installed in the toilets the forerunner of hot air hand dryers. They were big machines which had two nozzles and you could swirl one around. I remember one time, during the winter, when there were two old fellas who used to warm themselves up with them. They would direct the air on to their arms or drape their donkey jackets over the nozzles.

Eddie Jackson

I think we were our own worst enemy as regards safety. Just to get a job done quickly you would take a risk now and again.

Bob Seales

When you were on piece work, the safety element was thrown out of the window. All you were concerned about was getting the job done. I'm sorry to say there were a lot of accidents. It was only through

A welder at work in a precarious position in 1958.

diligent work through some certain shop stewards and of course the workforce that safety became a high priority.

Sometimes you would be working hundreds of feet up on a plank which was maybe only one or two feet wide. There would be no safety rail and nothing to grab on to. Gradually things began to change. Safety rails on staging were brought in and then safety nets were put inside tanks. If you were up on a crane, or anything like that, you would wear a wire harness. Despite these extra precautions there were still nasty accidents.

Then they started to look at the conditions within the yards. For example how quickly you could get to the men if they were hurt. An ambulance would sometimes have difficulty getting to the point of an accident as there was so much material lying around. Sometimes the only way to get an injured man out of the boat was by crane in a safety harness which isn't the ideal way to get him out. So improvements were made in that area as well.

Men used to paint the boats inside and out and knew very little about the contents of the paint they were using. During the early years there was a lot of people who suffered through their chests.

Ventilation was often poor. Men were on piece work and often wouldn't spend the time to set up a fan to take some of the fumes away from where they were working. That attitude applied to all the trades. The individual worker was often at fault because he didn't look after himself enough.

Mr Kiddy

On piece work the counter would come round and each work was measured. Then your pay was calculated. That's why you couldn't make you own tea – it was too expensive.

Jack Davitt

For many years men worked on single staging planks with no guard-rails or toe-boards sometimes eighty feet in the air. Behind them was nothing but space. In front of them the ship's hull curved inwards and downwards – away from where they were working and a fall usually ended on a pile of pipes or plates. When I was a young apprentice I

saw a driller fall about fifty feet from some staging to the ground. His drill had hit a hard bit in the shell and kicked back, throwing him off balance. A man nearby ran towards the driller and, as he did so, the pneumatic drill released itself and dropped also. It was on a length of pneumatic tubing which was just short of the ground. The machine fell, hit the second man on the head and then bounced up and down like a yo-yo on the tubing. Both men were seriously injured. The whole episode was quite unnecessary. If, as with housebuilding for example, there had been proper toe-boards and guard-rails the accident would never have happened.

Bill Purdie

Climbing about on the ships was an occupation in itself – the staging was sometimes terrible. It was nerve racking to walk along a thirty foot plank which was wobbling and there was no safety rail. It was even worse in the winter when everything had a covering of snow. I once saw a welder who had been working on the shell. He moved along to somewhere else and a plank came down right where he had been working.

Charles Thompson

When we were working in tanks or cargo holds where the lighting was very bad it was easy to have accidents. I've known men who thought they were stepping on to a plank when in fact it was just a shadow. You do something like that and the next thing you know you have fallen to the bottom of the hold.

R. Mather

During my apprenticeship I was told to file the rough edges from a recently burned hole in the shell of a ship. A grill was to be fitted over the intake of a pipe through which water would be sucked to go to the

circulating pump of the engine cooling system. The grill was to avoid sucking in seaweed, fish etc. The hole had been roughly cut by an acetylene burner and had a lot of razor-sharp appendages which had to be removed.

It was February and freezing cold. I had a thick woollen sweater under my boilersuit. I had kept my jacket on but by the time I had climbed the forty or so feet to the relevant single plank my hands were already numb. I started to file the hole and soon realised that some liquid was running down the file and staining my jacket. On further examination I discovered a long deep cut in my hand and was amazed to realise that I couldn't feel a thing. It was bleeding badly and so I decided to go to the Ambulance Room. I tried to pick up my tool bag to put the file back into it, to find that it had frozen to the plank and I had to kick it free.

I got my hand temporarily fixed and told my foreman that I had to go and get it stitched. I was very angry and told him it was an offence to human dignity to expect anyone to work in such circumstances and I was not prepared any longer to do it. I was so angry that the possible consequential termination of my apprenticeship never entered my head. To my surprise the foreman merely shrugged his shoulders and said, 'All right, I'll get somebody else to do it. There's a job in the machine shop I want doing. I'll tell you about it when you get back from the hospital.'

Bill Purdie

The last shipyard I worked in was in 1983. We were working on preparing the launch-ways underneath a ship. There was a new kind of paint being used and it was being sprayed on the ship. The paint was highly toxic. The rule in the yard was that if the painters came to the boat and started spraying you had to get out of the way. But I used to see shipwrights – my own trade – who would still work if the foreman was around and there were all these toxic fumes whizzing around. It just goes to show that even in 1983 there was the attitude of 'here's the gaffer I better be working.'

David Farquar

I was asked to work for eight weeks at Swan Hunter's by the BNA. I was quite anxious as I had never done any industrial nursing before. I shouldn't have worried as everyone was very friendly and keen to show me what to do and I picked the routine up very quickly. The injuries were fairly routine and I began recognising more and more faces around the yard, mainly through chatting to them when they came to the medical centre.

A welder at Swan's in the mid 1950s.

One incident occurred during my time at Swan's that I and everyone else there will never forget. A man fell off a ladder that was on the side of a ship, and suffered fatal injuries. The first-aiders and medical team were marvellous and everything possible was done. All the work stopped and a silence fell over the yard, it was an awful silence.

Men kept coming into the medical centre and were obviously shocked by what they had seen, they needed a lot of reassurance. The radios were buzzing with messages regarding the incident and I felt helpless listening to them.

Everyone at the yard was upset and everyone was thinking of his family. I was touched by the strength of feeling amongst the work-force. I will always remember my short time there, and feel sorry that I will never get the chance to go back.

Linda Wilson (Relief Nurse)

At one time, welders used to have special permits which allowed them to get milk. It was supposed to help them overcome the fumes they worked in.

Maurice Wakefield

If you were working in the double bottoms or the coffer dam it was thick with fumes all day long because of the welders.

Charles Thompson

They brought in extraction in about 1969-70. It was because we were using new welding rods which were very small and very smoky. Everyone was up in arms about it. There was a big mass meeting and thousands of shipyard workers threatened to go on strike and so they had to bring in proper extraction. These were extractor fans to suck the fumes off. But again if people wanted to get their work done they just generally ignored it. Most welders were told to make sure they had outside extractors. I always used one.

Tony Parker

I was a welder and spent all my working life in terrible conditions. Wherever you were inside a ship you were working in welding fumes but when you got down to the bottom, and coffer dams and bulbous bows, the conditions were atrocious – you could hardly see because the fumes were so thick. People who have never seen such conditions wouldn't believe how bad they were. We fought for better conditions for years, and eventually they started getting them as the shipyards were finishing.

When I started serving my time in the 1940s, your protective clothing consisted of gloves and that was it – a pair of gloves and nothing else. Of course you had a welder's screen of blue glass but that was so you could weld, not to protect your eyes. It was just so you could do your job and see what you were welding. Later we got leather aprons and leather gauntlets, helmets and safety boots.

We had to fight hard to get extractors for the fumes, but we got them in the end. When I first started to serve my time I would pinch riveters 'windy' pipes – their compressed air pipes – to try to blow fumes away. Then some big brawny riveter would come and grab you because you've got his windy pipe.

Jack Davitt

Asbestos used to be everywhere. I used to work in the engine rooms of the ships – particularly the Admiralty ships – and I would come out looking like a miller. At that time most people didn't know the dangers of asbestos. I was very ignorant.

Maurice Wakefield

When I was seventeen or eighteen I was working in compartments where men were spraying blue asbestos out of a three inch nozzle on to all the bulkheads, shelves and everywhere else. We were working amongst all this and didn't know it would do us any harm. I have lost a lot of friends who have died from asbestosis.

Allan Blackett

I can mind as a bairn – when I was seventeen – I was working on the flooring of an engine room. Above us there were some men lagging steam pipes with asbestos. They were sawing chunks off the asbestos so that it would fit the bends in the pipes. The asbestos was floating down on to us like snowflakes. We were there all day and when we came out we looked like snowmen because there was so much asbestos on us.

Dick Flemming

I was a driller and at one time we had to drill into asbestos sheets – but we weren't told what it was. The asbestos was all flaking off and we were breathing in all this dust. No-one told us of the dangers then.

John Geddes

In the late 1960s, when I was eighteen, I was working on some ferries and they were spraying wet asbestos on the bulkheads to fire-proof them. It must have been three inches thick and everywhere was covered in white dust. It was just floating around the ships like snow. Looking back, I can't believe how they could let that happen.

Tony Parker

Vessel One-O-Nine
by Ripyard Cuddling

The Winter chill has reached the Tyne
It's cold on Vessel-One-O-Nine
And workers huddle close together
Against the grim December weather.

Woolly hats and duffel coats
Mufflers wrapped around our throats
Tears in eyes and drops on noses
Cheeks as red as Summer roses.

Ice upon the staging planks
Snow that drifts into the tanks
Managers with Winter faces
Shelter in their warm oasis.

Tattered gloves and boots that leak
Frozen bones that groan and creek
Fingers stiff too numb to grip
It's cold aboard this cursed ship.

Dreaming in our confined spaces
Of bluer skies and better places
Dreams of pleasures out of reach
Like deck chairs on a Spanish beach.

Weary mornings tired nights
Rain that clings and frost that bites
Fog advancing cold and dank
Blotting out the shipyard bank.

Muffled oaths from frozen lips
Foremen wielding verbal whips
Foghorns wail their sad lament
And speak to me of discontent.

Amidst it all I stand and shiver
And gaze across the icy river
And search for words inside my head
One day my story may be read.

And as my poem nears its end
With word I hop will rhyme and blend
You may have guessed the final line …
It's cold on vessel One-O-Nine.

SECTION FOUR

WOMEN WORKERS

In the Shell Shop of Swan, Hunter & Wigham
Richardson during the First World War.

The *Shipyard Magazine* of February 1919 published the following article about a party for those who had worked in the Shell Shop during the First World War:

On Saturday, December 7th, 1918, there took place a most interesting function in the Heaton Assembly Rooms, in connection with the firm of Messrs Swan, Hunter & Wigham Richardson Ltd.

The work in the Shell Shop of the firm having come to an end, by the termination of hostilities, a farewell party was kindly given by the Directors and Management of the Neptune Works to the girls and men who for the last three years have laboured to turn out ammunition for our forces abroad.

The invitations were from 3 to 6.30, and after a sumptuous tea, to which everyone did full justice, an adjournment was made to the ballroom, where the most interesting ceremony of the afternoon took place. The chair was taken by G. Vardy Esq, and on the platform were Lady Hunter, Mr and Mrs G.F. Tweedy, Captain J.H. Bruce (Engineer and Secretary of the local Board of Management of the Ministry of Munitions) and Mrs Bruce, Captain Thorne, Mr and Mrs Yates, Miss Harvey, Mr and Mrs Morgan and others.

The Chairman first expressed the regrets of Sir G.B. Hunter and Mr and Mrs Denham Christie, who were unable to be present. After welcoming guests, he said that they were met together on this auspicious occasion to say farewell, after being closely associated for almost the whole period of the War. He wished to take the opportunity, on behalf of the workers – the girls and women particularly – for the excellent work they had done during that long time. He emphasised the appreciation of the Directors and Management at the good feeling and *esprit de corps* that had always existed in the Shell Shop.

In conclusion, he had the pleasant duty to perform, to call upon Mrs Tweedy to present momentoes to seven of the women workers whose names had been chosen from the records kept of their work; also to six women workers who had been in the Shell Shop from the commencement. The presents, which consisted of gold bracelets (with inscriptions) for the first seven and gold bar brooches for the second number (whose names were chosen by the firm), were kindly given by G.F. Tweedy, Esq, one of the Directors. Mrs Tweedy then made the presentations amidst much applause.

Mr Tweedy, responding on Mrs Tweedy's behalf, said how pleased he was to have the opportunity of meeting them all once more. Their labours had come to an end, and it would no doubt be a source of gratification to them all to remember in the years to come that their individual efforts had helped to win the war. He wished them all 'good luck'. He had heard that many of the girls had lost their war badges, and he hoped that when they received permission from the Minister of Munitions to retain their war badges they would all be able to remember the different places wherein they had mislaid them. (Loud applause.)

Mr Yates, manager of the Shell Shop, then spoke, giving a brief resume of the work done since the commencement of the shop, and then proposed a hearty vote of thanks to Mr and Mrs Tweddy for their kindness and generosity, which was seconded by Miss Nicholson and carried with acclamation. The remainder of the afternoon was passed in dancing interspersed with songs.

The following is a list of the recipients who received presentations: Mrs Willis, Miss J. Bell, Miss E. Maston, Miss D. Nicholson, Miss E. Hanson, Miss V, Browning, Miss S. Hatfield, Miss M. Patton, Miss L. Pearson, Miss E. McGeary, Miss E. Morrill, Miss I. Heslop, Miss S. Armstrong and Miss A. Richardson.

Two interesting presentations took place on the evening of December 23rd, 1918, at the Neptune Works, when Miss Harvey, the chief Welfare Supervisor, and Mrs Quinn, the Shipyard Forewoman, were the recipients of very handsome presents from the girls employed in the Shipyard Department.

The donors had taken this opportunity for their presentation, as they all felt that the time was shortly coming when they would be asked to give up their work to the returning soldiers, and they might not be able to all meet together again. Miss Harvey received a silver and tortoise shell inlaid box and Mrs Quinn a silver-plated tea service.

The presentations were made in the girls' messroom, which had been gaily decorated for the occasion, and later an excellent tea was served. The rest of the evening was spent in dancing.

Women workers in a north-east shipyard.

I went to work in the shipyards because I wanted to do my bit for the war effort. I was working in a fruit shop when I heard that some of my friends had gone to work at Palmer's at Hebburn. In 1939 I went down to Hebburn and had an interview. I was asked why I wanted to work in a dirty shipyard. I said I was too young to join the forces – I was 14$^{1}/_{2}$ at the time – but still wanted to do 'my bit'. They took me on as a rivet catcher. I found that very boring and I left after about nine months. I went to the Labour Exchange in Hebburn and told them I was sick of my job and wanted to work somewhere else.

I then started at Swan Hunter's, learning tack welding in the Training School. I was there about six weeks learning the basics. They taught us how to weld – but not like the lads who had served their time. We were just filling in really. I stayed at Swan's until the end of the war and I really enjoyed my time there.

Alice Thompson

I was working as a waitress in Carricks and the Imperial Hotel when the war broke out. My three brothers were away in the Navy and so my father wouldn't let me go away from home. At that time you either had to join the Forces, the Land Army or work in a munitions factory. Well the shipyard was the nearest to where I lived so I went into the yards. I started work in a shed in the yard where I did my training. I started in 1942 and was one of the first batch there. They would take about eight or ten at a time and with me were some good girls and we had a lot of fun. But mind you we had to graft when there was work to do.

Mary Fraser

Women did not only work in shipyards during wartime. Here are tracers at their desks.

I started at Swan Hunter's in 1940. My mam wouldn't let me join the Land Army or work in a munitions factory, so I went to work in the shipyard. I started as a cleaner – sweeping up on the boats. I was 17 or 18 at the time. My dad worked there, he was a slinger on the cranes. Also my future father-in-law worked with the caulkers. Two of my friends worked in Swan's and it was they who suggested I should join them. 'Why don't you try – it's marvellous money.' I suppose it was good money for those days. My dad went to see the person responsible for taking people on. He asked how old I was and a few other questions and then he said to my dad, 'Tell the bairn to come down. She can start in the morning.' Not next week – the next morning!

Not long after I started, I was given a 'blue-eyed-job', working the lift on the aircraft carrier *Albion*. The lift had a handle which operated it. If I needed to go to the loo while I was working I would take the handle with me. When I got back there were sometimes men waiting to use the lift. They would say, 'Where the hell have you been?' But they couldn't use the lift without me.

Irene Wonders

They used to say that the women working in the yards were 'common'. So we didn't tell people where we worked. My parents were frightened in case anything happened to me in the yards.

Audrey Nichols

In those days people thought that 'nice' women didn't work in shipyards. I was going out with a boy at the time and he used to say to me, 'Don't ever tell anyone that you work in a shipyard.' Well, I didn't see anything wrong in it. The funny thing was he worked in the same yard as me. I thought if you don't like me working in the yard – and if you're ashamed of me – I don't want to go out with you any more. So I chucked him.

Alice Thompson

The men treated us with a lot of respect and I never heard any bad language. It wasn't what we were expecting. The men curbed their tongues when we were working with them. They were very kind and it was fun to work together. Most of the men were a lot older than me and they looked after me. I would be made cups of tea and I was spoilt really.

Audrey Nichols

When I first started work I was frightened by the sheer size of the ships. Sometimes we were working on decks that had open spaces and you had to walk along a narrow plank to get to your job. When I first saw what I was expected to walk along I refused and said I couldn't even crawl across that. The lads I was working with said, 'You want a dance floor, you,' and fetched some more planks.

Mary Fraser

Some of them treated me like a daughter. They would say, 'I wouldn't let my daughter work here.' I suppose the men were surprised to see women working in the yards. But once they saw that you could do your job they came to terms with it and we were accepted. I knew I had to prove to the lads that I could do a good job because if they thought you couldn't do it, they would have nothing to do with you. Maybe they would go to their foreman and say, 'We don't want her, she won't do her job properly. She's always running off to the rest room and leaving her job.' So they would ask someone else to take her place. But that never happened to me and I more or less worked with the same fella all the time I worked there.

Alice Thompson

The Tyne at Bill Quay 55.

I was terrified when I first went into the yard – it was so huge. But after half an hour it was as if you had worked there all your life because the people were so kind. The men I worked with were super. If they swore in front of me, they would always say, 'Sorry pet, I didn't know you were there.' Our forelady used to say, 'You understand how men swear. But if it's not said at you, just ignore it.' Which we did. But there was very little swearing really, they were real gentlemen.

Irene Wonders

I thought the language of the men was disgusting. So I went to the gaffer and said, 'I'm not working with them.' Then they put notices up saying, 'Women – no bad language.' Apart from that I enjoyed the work.

Mary Fraser

I found the men to be very courteous. Most of the men were just lads really – between the ages of 15 and 19. The other men were a lot older. They were men who were too old to be called up into the Forces. I would go to the pictures and dances with the younger lads. But there were some women, the older ones, who would go drinking and play darts. I used to think that was terrible.

Alice Thompson

I was paid £8 15s 0d when I was on 'piece' work, which I thought was a fortune. Later, when I was married, my husband and I only had just over £4 a week to live on. I was paid off when I was 21 because then

PELAW MAIN   N°7

you started to be paid big money. At that time the war was coming to an end and I suppose it was thought the men would be coming back. Soon they starting paying-off the women. I was released overnight and didn't have time to say good-bye to my friends. I didn't want to leave and there were tears in my eyes when I was let go. I'll never forget the war years – for me they were happy memories. They were some sad times as well but they were happy days.

Audrey Nichols

When I first started I was on 7s 6d. Each year you got older you got a little bit more – you got a rise with each birthday. In those days you started work at half past seven in the morning and worked till quarter past five. We also worked from half past seven till 12 o'clock on a Saturday. So we worked a 48 hour week. We could work overtime on a Tuesday and a Thursday until about seven o'clock and also on a Saturday afternoon and a Sunday. If you worked all those days you could earn good money. Well, at that time my father had been called up into the Army, and there was only me and my two younger brothers at home. So I used to work all the hours I could to get money for my mam. But I liked my job so it wasn't a great hardship for me.

I was about 18 when I started coming on to what I called the big money – although it was still a lot less than the men. I used to come home with about £4 19s 0d. Of course I was working all hours God sent. But I was so proud to take all that money home to mam.

We never got the same money as men. I sometimes wished I could get the same as them but then again they did do a harder job than me. They also had more experience than I did. But after doing my job for three years I thought I should have been on the same wage.

Alice Thompson

When a ship was nearing completion the head cleaning lady, would take all of us cleaners on board. There would be about 50 of us. We would scrub all the cabins out with naphtha and wire wool and polish all the port holes and everything else. It would look lovely when it was finished – you couldn't believe how it looked. They were like new pins, they were beautiful.

Irene Wonders

I worked on the aircraft carrier *Leviathan*. The Duchess of Kent, who was a real lady, launched her and there were lots of other 'big wigs' like the mayor. It was a superb ship, really beautiful, and I loved working on her. I was proud that I had done my little bit to help build that ship. When the *Leviathan* left I was crying.

Audrey Nichols

Towards the end of the war we started building these long things with flat bottoms and no-one could understand what they were – they were like big barges. Obviously the foremen, and others high up, knew what we were making but they wouldn't let on. Then one day I went to the pictures and the newsreel was showing the 'D' Day landings at Normandy. I was sitting there and saw on the screen the barges which we had built. I felt so proud that I had done my little bit for the war effort.

Alice Thompson

Once there was an air-raid and we all went on to a battleship to take cover. We were on the ship a long time and we were all having a sing-song when the 'all-clear' was sounded. We were enjoying ourselves. I suppose when you are young you don't have much fear.

Audrey Nichols

The women had a rest room with a lady attendant who would make tea. At about 10 o'clock, if we weren't too busy, I would be told to have a break. I would go to the rest room and buy a cup of tea. There were also toilets and wash basins in the rest room. It was nice and private and it was a good place to go to if you needed to get away for a few minutes. It was also a place to see your friends and have a little natter. Some of the women used to also have a cigarette there as well.

Alice Thompson

My dad had told me about the rats in the yards. When my mam used to put his bait up, she used to say, 'Do you want spam or cheese, Harry?' 'It doesn't matter,' he would say, 'The rats will eat owt.'

On my first day at Swan's, I went to see my dad at dinner time. I was sitting next to him and he says, 'Just sit still hinney, just sit still.' Then out of this hole poked a nose, then more and more of the rat's body poked out of the hole. I thought it was frightening but my dad told me, 'It's all right, it'll not come closer than that.' Then one of my dad's friends throws a bit bait down and all of a sudden five or six rats came scrabbling over the first one to get at the food.

Later, when I was cleaning the ships, if I had to go into somewhere dark you always thought there would be rats around, so I would always bang my brush down a few times to give them a chance to run away. It was an experience I will never forget.

Irene Wonders

I suffered a few times from 'flashes'. When it happened I tried a few different remedies. There was one old welder (I'm saying old – he must have been about in his late forties) who said to me, 'The best remedy is to put raw sliced potato on each eye and lie down in a dark room until it gets better.' I tried it and it worked – it was very soothing.

Alice Thompson

Some of the lads were a bit rough but outside the yards, if they took you to dances and such like, they treated you like a lady. But at work the lads could play some tricks. The tricks the lads played were never dirty tricks – just mischievous. One day they put my feet and hands in some stocks and stuck me outside the gaffer's door while they ran off. Another day they tied me up like a mummy and put me on a crate. They all ran away when the gaffer came along and he had to get me down. He said, 'If you had been a laddie I would have put a foot up your backside.'

Mary Fraser

All the women who were my age – the young 'uns – got on very well. The older ones – in their 30s and 40s – didn't bother with us. Because we were so young we would have some daft ideas. There was three of us who said that after the war we would all meet in New York on the steps of the Statue of Liberty on a certain date. I mean it sounds ridiculous now, but at the time we were very serious about it.

Alice Thompson

ODD TALES

I laugh at Billy Connelly's humour. He worked in a shipyard in Glasgow and he once said that his humour isn't Scottish or English it's shipyard humour. Whenever I hear him I just roll up laughing because I can identify with his stories and his jokes.

Malcolm Scott

It wasn't a joy to go to work – especially in winter – but a little bit of carry on amongst ourselves helped to lighten the day a little bit. We went through a phase where everyone talked to each like the children's TV show *The Clangers*. Then another time we would extend our measuring tape and pretend to talk to someone like it was a walkie-talkie. It was often just silly things like that which went on.

Bob Seales

There were lots of eccentrics in the yards. There was one old fella, a tiny man who was 5 foot 2 inches at the most – but you imagined he was smaller than that. He had this huge pedal cycle which took a great effort to ride. At the time there was a cowboy film out – with someone like Gary Cooper – called 'Tall in the Saddle'. So the next time the fella rode past on his bike someone shouted, 'Here comes Tall in the Saddle.' The name stuck until he left.

Eddie Jackson

There was one character called the 'Gateshead Burglar'. Some people also called him the 'Barber's Enemy' because he always wanted a haircut. I was working at Hawthorn Leslie's, in the days when we worked piece work, and the Gateshead Burglar was working there as well. There was a really good job going – which was good money – and me and my mate were going to do it. We got out our gear, and were just about to start, then the Gateshead Burglar came along and said, 'You're wanted, you two, in the foreman's office straightaway – immediately.' So off we went to the foreman's office across the yard. But when we got to his office we found that he didn't want us. While we were away the Gateshead Burglar welded our job. That's how he got his name.

Jack Davitt

One manager was called 'Mr 19 plus' because he used to come round every twenty minutes. Then there was 'Puck' – after Puck matches – because he was very tall and slim and always wore a red helmet. The 'Sheriff' used to come round and say, 'Where's the hold up, where's the hold up?' And the 'Paratrooper' would say, 'I've just dropped in.' One man who thought if he didn't say anything he wouldn't get a nickname was called 'The Dolly'.

Hugh Archibold

There was one lad who used to file his false teeth in a vice at work. He used to say they weren't fitting his gums properly. But he wouldn't go to the dentists to have a bit scraped off. I think at the finish he had filed so much off that when he talked his teeth would fall out. When he retired the lads made him a proper presentation case with a set of his old false teeth in it and some very small files.

Bob Seales

One of the lads who was on night shift, which started at half past seven, wanted to see Newcastle play under floodlights and asked the gaffer if it was all right if he came in late. The gaffer, who thought he would be in before 10 o'clock, said it was OK and told him to report to the gate house when he came in. What he didn't tell him was that Newcastle were playing at Leeds that night so he didn't come in until 2 o'clock in the morning. The gaffer ended up in front of the management for allowing someone to come in so late.

Aidan Nicholson

The working man always finds a way to beat the gaffer. It's like when you were in the Army you had to beat the sergeant. You always have to find a way of beating the system.

Allan Blackett

When a ship was on the stocks you used to get on board by using a spiral gangway. These were terrible if you were carrying heavy gear. When we started building supertankers there was no way you could get on and off using a gangway like this and so lifts were installed. I remember one day me and Neville Taylor, a foreman welder, were waiting for the lift to come down from one of these supertankers. We waited and waited and eventually it came down. There was only one man in that lift and it was the Shipyard Padre. Nev said to me, 'I knew the lift went high, but I didn't know it went that high.'

Jack Davitt

There was a shipwright who was poorly so one of the lads said to him, 'You want to get yersel a bottle of Guinness.' A fortnight later the two met up again and the lad said, 'How are you getting on with the Guinness.'

In the Joiners' Shop

The shipwright says, 'It doesn't half take some getting through taken a spoonful at a time.'

David Farquar

There was one squad, the red-leaders who put the first rust-inhibiting coat of paint on the bare steel hull, who were distinguishable by the fact that they were invariably covered from head to foot in red lead paint. Not only the decks, bulkheads, frames etc got covered in the stuff – but also themselves. They were on piece work so the sooner they got the job completed the sooner they got paid. When they were operating it was fatal to leave a jacket hanging on a bulkhead because they just painted right over it. This was long before the sophistication of paint sprayers or even rollers and the red-leaders just used big brushes and huge cans of smelly, very adhesive, revolting dull red paint which they applied to everything that didn't get out of their way.

Bill Purdie

One lad who worked on the lathes once brought a ham shank into work. He put the meat into his boilersuit with bits of meat hanging out. He then knocks on the door of the foreman who was getting on a bit and nearing retirement. The lad said to the foreman, 'Get me an ambulance – I've had an accident.' The foreman threw a right wobbler.

Aidan Nicholson

In the drawing office we used art gum for cleaning up the pencil work drawings. Sometimes we used to crumble it up and mix it with someone's baccy. The stench was terrible.

Eddie Jackson

The door of the toilet cubicles had a big gap at the bottom. One day a group of apprentices put a pair of old boots under each toilet door – there were about 20 of them. All you could see when you walked into the toilets were all the doors closed and boots underneath. When the men found out what had happened there was nearly a riot.

Jack Davitt

The practical jokes weren't too funny if you were on the receiving end. A lot of people were very cruel to the apprentices. The older fellas would sometimes get the young lads who had teddyboy haircuts and cut off their quiffs and stick them on the wall. Along a joiner's bench you would have all these big Tony Curtis quiffs. I've seen rough necked teddyboys in tears because they couldn't take it.

Malcolm Scott

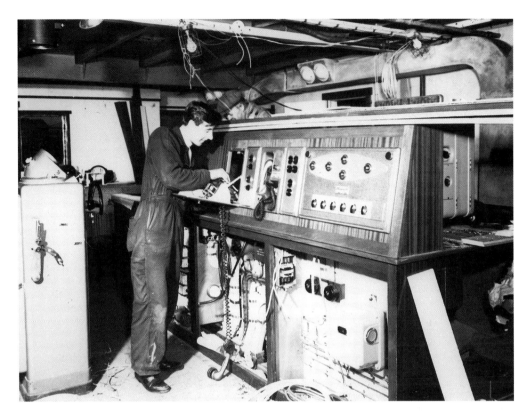

Shiprepair yards were very different places to work – you had a different breed of blokes who worked there. They often didn't give a 'monkeys' because they were only working there a few weeks at a time – that was the nature of the work. In the yards you knew you were there for years so you had to behave yourself.

Aidan Nicholson

In the 1930s some chargehands and foremen wore safety boots which, in those days, were large, clumsy and had steel tips on their heels. Now welding had just come into fashion and one of the standard tricks was to occupy the attention of them whilst an apprentice tacked the steel heelplates to the deck – and when the foreman tried to approach the lads the effect was startling.

These safety boots were a Godsend in some ways not intended by the makers. There was a story about one foreman who entered a compartment and found the men playing cards. 'Why is it,' he demanded, 'that every time I come in here I find you lot playing cards instead of working?'

There was a pause then one of them said, 'Well, it's because you stopped wearing your safety boots and started wearing those crepe-soled shoes!'

Bill Purdie

Sir John Hunter would take people round the yard – particularly the Japanese – and he would end his grand tour with a sweep of his hands and he would say, 'Gentleman, here is the end of the Roman wall.' But when they altered the yard these stones were removed. So one day when he went round the yard he said, 'Here is the end of the … my God where have they gone?' We had to quickly find some stones and put them back. They are still there to this day to mark the end of the wall.

Hugh Archibold

Colonel Pickby used to ride down from Jesmond on his horse. His groom would come down by tram and would be at the yard in time for the Colonel to arrive.

Harry - an engineer 1917-23 and 36-37

If Colonel Pickby saw you with your hands in your pocket – even on a dinnertime – he would nail you straightaway: 'Get your hands out of your pockets and straighten your back, son,' he would bark.

Albert Buckton

As part of our training we made pokers. Nearly every home had a poker that was made at work. I don't think there was an apprentice who didn't make one. You made at least one and maybe got orders from your aunts or others in your family.

There were lots of other things made – sledges, rakes, trowels and one lad actually made a wheel-barrow.

Aidan Nicholson

One Christmas all the lads took a bit of tinsel into work and we hung it around a panel which had all flashing lights on it. That was our Christmas tree. Another year a lad brought a Christmas tree in – I don't know how he got through the gate with it. We were in porter cabins along the jetty and we put the tree up and decorated it with nuts and bolts.

Bob Seales

I've seen people make coffee tables, wardrobes and chest of drawers in the yards and then sneak them out. It was like those films about prisoners of war who are trying to fool the Germans. I remember a time when one lad wore a big coat and underneath he had a chest of drawers hanging from a rope around his neck. He then got five or six of his friends around him as he walked out of the gate. Once he was past the guards on the gate he was straight up to Wallsend Station.

Malcolm Scott

Maurice The Polis would stand by the gate before the buzzer sounded. He was a big fella and he would stand as if he was on parade. He would parade backwards and forwards attempting to keep the men back. But as the buzzer went he had to get out the way sharpish because everyone was gannin' so quick.

Leslie Took

In the 1950s, when we left at 5.30 I've seen men fall and be trampled running up that bank. We had to run up the bank because no-one had cars and so you rushed up to get on the train or bus before everyone else. You could either get the early train at the riverside or the later train at Wallsend. The riverside train used to run right through Swan Hunter's. We used to get workman's tickets then. We would buy them on a night to save time the following morning. I would ask for 'two workman's for tomorrow'.

Malcolm Scott

I used to travel from South Shields to Wallsend. I would catch the Mid Tyne Ferry by Hawthorn Leslie's. It was sometimes an adventure going across on the ferry, especially before they glazed the sides in. Before that there were just rails and as it was approaching the ferry landing people used to climb on the other side of the rails and stand on what

was called the running board (the fender) to get a quick getaway. They would leap off as soon as the ferry was near the landing. I remember one time when an old fella took a step off too early and went straight into the water. Straight away there were about twenty hands in the water trying to catch him while about another 40 were keeping the ferry off the sides. The bloke was out in a second. That's what it was like – you looked after your fellow man.

Eddie Jackson

When the sheds were developed there was a major problem with starlings. Hundreds of birds rousted in the roof and they bred up there as well. It became a major problem – for example it became very slippy with so much bird droppings on the ground. During the day it wasn't too bad because the noise of the yard kept the birds away but when the noise abated they came back. A few things were tried to get rid of them. First, the yard manager sent someone up with a piece of steel to bang and make as much noise as he could to scare away the birds. It didn't make much difference – they just went from one end to the other and eventually came back when he stopped. There was a manager who was into hunting, shooting and fishing and he brought his shotgun into the yard and he had a go at them. But he only got about one in every hundred. Next firecrackers were put on to the beams and set off – but that didn't have much effect. There were even loudspeakers set up with a recording of a starling being slowly strangled – but the birds seemed to enjoy it. Eventually they found out how to get rid of the starlings – they pulled the sheds down. It goes to show how nature can defeat the best efforts of man.

Hugh Archibold

The sports ground in Wallsend used to be superb. The pitches were the best drained fields in the area. We never had to cancel matches. There was, in the old days, Works Sports Days – A bit like School Sports Days. One of the sports they played was 'Fives' which was a very aristocratic game for a shipyard.

Eddie Jackson

The main jetty at Swan Hunter's was built over the outfalls of four large open sewers and raw untreated sewage was evacuated into the river. The assumption was that it would be swept out to sea. Unfortunately the speed of the river had slowed to the extent that before the sewage could indeed be swept out to sea the tide changed and it all got swept back up the river. It was said that if you fell into the Tyne you didn't die from drowning but from poisoning instead.

After a ship was launched it spent months at the main jetty being 'fitted out' – i.e. being converted from a steel box into a finished vessel. It took a long time to out-fit a liner or a warship and, as a consequence, they had to be put into a dry dock and their bottoms scraped free of the accumulated sewage before they could have their hulls finally painted. The state of the river water was indescribable and at low tide, when the water level was below the levels of the outlets, the stench was ghastly.

During the Second World War there was an incident which could only have happened under such extraordinary conditions. A battleship was being completed and, because of its size and draught, it was moored about twenty feet away from the jetty in deeper water. There were pontoons keeping the ship away from the jetty and a number of gangways for access. Because it had a heavily armoured weather deck it was decided that in the event of an air raid workers should board the ship and go below this deck for safety.

One dark night the Germans decided to raid Glasgow and came over Tyneside. Now the Army had, at intervals of about ten yards down each side of the river, crude smoke-producing furnaces which burned very dirty, residual, crude oil which produced thick clouds of smoke which was blown by the wind across the river hopefully obscuring it and confusing the intruding German navigators. On this night, despite the fact there was no moon, the Army lit all their smoke producers and the fog they created on the river made the pitch-black even darker. During the day some of the access gangways had been shifted to other positions and some of the nightshift on hearing the warning sirens raced down to where the gangways had been, and in their panic went over the edge into the river. They were there for some time, clinging to the pontoons before their cries attracted attention and they were hauled out. They sat in the Ambulance Room while their clothes were dried out and then refused to put them back on because of the smell. The Ambulance Room itself had to be fumigated and the men sent home by ambulance wearing only blankets. They were ever after known as 'the stinkers'. Three of them ended up in hospital with unknown poisoning and spent weeks in recovery not so much from being immersed but from what they were immersed in.

Bill Purdie

In 1940 I started my first year of apprenticeship as a welder at the age of 16. The welding department at that time was governed by the head foreman welder, Davy Lamb. Davy was a benevolent, uncle-like figure who ruled with a velvet glove or at least that was the impression he tried to put over. His second in command was Joe Mills. Joe looked as hard as nails and indeed was as hard as nails. Between them they ran the welding department in a Jekyll and Hyde kind of way. Welders

A diesel shunter propels a wagon of steel plates into Swan's in 1980.

worked strict piece work and they really did work like slaves from the gates opening to the homeward trek at night. The drinking of tea was strictly forbidden by management under the threat of all kinds of punishment, but to the hard working shipyard worker the 9 o'clock break for 'bait' was a must and looking back I'm sure a lot of managerial eyes turned the other way when tools were downed for the ten minute break each morning.

The journeyman welders would recruit an apprentice to make their cans of tea. I was commissioned by three welders to make theirs for a small fee. There were absolutely no facilities for making tea so the cans had to be boiled on a rivet heater's fire. The rivet maker was bribed with a Woodbine for the use of his fire. On one particular occasion I was caught by a 'toot'. A toot was a plain clothes security agent whose job was to get workers sacked for carrying out these kinds of duties.

In due course I was summoned to the head foreman's office to explain my crime. I knocked on the door and after a long and soul destroying wait I was bid 'Enter'. What happened next could have come straight from the pages of Dickens. Davy Lamb sat behind his desk looking very grim and in a corner behind a cloud of Woodbine smoke sat the dreaded Joe Mills. 'Now you know, son,' said Davy. 'I can't have apprentices running round the yard making tea. This is a very serious offence and I'm trying to sort out what to do with you.'

'Sack him,' called Joe Mills. 'Sack him.'

I was wondering if it would help my case if I took my cap off, but decided against it. The truth was I was too terrified to move.

'Now Joe,' he said. 'I think we'll give the lad one more chance,' and turning to me he said, 'I'm going to fine you one shilling. It will be deducted from your wages, and if you're caught doing it again I'm going to take Mr Mill's advice.' I tottered out of the office back to my job.

The three welders who employed me to make their tea gave me 6d each when they heard of my punishment so that was the fine paid and 6d into my pocket. I was now regarded as something of a hero by the other apprentice welders having been in the 'Lions' Den' and came out showing a profit.

Looking back on my trial, however, I often wonder if the two foremen were as formidable as they made themselves out to be. On recollection, as I left, I remember hearing Joe Mills growl, 'You should have sacked him Davy.' But from the corner of my eye I saw him give a sly wink, and Davy's shoulders seemed to be shaking in a most un-foremanlike manner.

Jack Davitt

The morning tea break was like the Japanese tea ceremony. Lots of blokes would have a baby's milk tin with a wire handle on it. They would send one of the young lads to fill it from the boiler. Tea would be brought in a piece of newspaper in your pocket. The men would get the paper out, unfold it and swill it around the water. You'd see all these guys standing in the sheds waving these big tins around. Other people would bring in old army canteens with a tin cup on the top – these would all come out at tea break.

Tony Parker

When the shipbuilding industry was nationalised in 1977 the *Evening Chronicle* reported Ripyard Cuddling's thoughts of the dawn of a new era:

Rum all round?

Free beer and rum when we're Government run says shipyard poet Ripyard Cuddling. Celebrations are in store lads for 'when we reach that magic day our troubles will be swept away.' So writes Ripyard after working for 37 years in the Tyneside yards, which tomorrow become part of Britain's nationalised shipbuilding industry. But behind the pen 52-year-old welder John Davitt of Whitley Road, Hollystone, is not so sure.

'Perhaps we will get better working conditions and more redundancy money but that's all. Nothing will really change, certainly not the blokes themselves,' he said.

But John still has his dreams. As Ripyard Cuddling he sees an end to shipyard muddling and the workers world put to rights.

> The wages for the shipyard force,
> Will double every month of course;
> Large bonuses and other things,
> Will help us all live like Kings.
> In every yard beside the gate.
> A cafe for the workers' bait;
> And to keep them all in peak condition,
> Free pints of Bass and Exhibition.
> In winter when the frosts are hard,
> The Government will give each yard,
> A glass of rum for every person,
> And double if conditions worsen.
> Conditions will improve tenfold.
> Our pockets will be lined with gold;
> As wealthy as the richest docker,
> And I might even get a locker.

I can't remember a time when I didn't write poems. I used to write them at school but I didn't show them to anyone. I used to throw them on the fire. It was only sissies that wrote poems. I used to like to play football, and rough and tumble, but I used to write poetry as well. I wrote some in the Navy and then later when I was back in the shipyards. I was working at the Naval Yard at Walker and there was supposed to be a ban on overtime and then a rumour was spread around that Sunday was on for certain people. This rumour was spread until it reached one fella's ear. He came to work on this Sunday morning with a big bag of bait. He went down the bank and he was the only one there. So I wrote a poem about him – and that's where it all started.

Jack Davitt

Every time Jack wrote a new poem it was put on the notice board. Jack had a good talent for reflecting what people thought. There was one poem about winter on the deck which was spot on. His poems were humorous in the sense that he knew what it was like to work in a shipyard.

Tony Parker

There were super artists in all the yards. Many were untrained. A plater, Peter Burns, was sponsored by the firm to do shipyard scenes. He also did a lot of portraits, almost caricatures. They were larger than life as well. I remember the first time he exhibited. All we had was a slip of paper with the title 'Old Boots' in biro. (Everybody called ball-point pens biros in those days.) We were expecting this little sketch in biro about 8" x 8" of a pair of old boots. When it arrived it was 4' x 4'. The boots were 2' 6" long. And it was in biro. Peter always went for real character and exaggeration. He was really good.

The exhibition was very successful. Others were held all over, including Newcastle Central Library and North Shields Library. Sometimes there were three exhibitions a year.

Eddie Jackson

SECTION SIX

THE SAVE OUR SWANS CAMPAIGN

In May 1993 Swan Hunter's went into receivership – the campaign to save the yard began.

We were waiting and waiting for the order for the helicopter carrier. We had put all our eggs in one basket in the hope of winning the order and so when it went to the Barrow shipyard it was devastating. I was a supervisor at the time and the day after the news was announced I was called into the manager's office. I was told in no uncertain terms that an announcement would be made that day about what was going to happen. I was informed that the receivers were coming in. I went on to the shop floor and said to the men at half past seven in the morning what was happening. There were grown men crying that day.

At half past twelve, when it was officially announced that the liquidators would be coming in, we sat around talking and trying to calm each other down. A lot of men were married, they had mortgages and families and as I was a supervisor it was my job to help them. I had been with the company for 20 years and been through some tough times but that day was the hardest I had been through. It will stick in my mind for the rest of my life.

After that it was a question of waiting to find out what was happening to our future – which was very hard. You had to continue working but nobody was really interested. You couldn't motivate people. I couldn't motivate myself so there was no way I could motivate people in the pipe factory where I worked.

There was always rumours going around the place that we were going to close. At the beginning of June it was announced that there was going to be 420 redundancies and, not knowing who or where they would come from, we waited.

Then, one morning, I was told at half past seven that we would be losing three men out of the pipe factory. One was a painter who had been with the company for over thirty years. He was only about forty-nine but being a painter had really affected him and he looked around seventy. They had chosen ten managers to go around that day and tell 420 men they were no longer required. That morning I was handed a bit of paper with three names on it and asked if I could bring them to the main office one at a time to be told. So I went to see the painter and said, 'Look, we've got some bad news for you. I can come in with you when you go in to get counselled by the managers or you can go in by yourself.' That lad wanted me to go in with him and I sat there and listened to him be told that after thirty years he was leaving the industry with nothing. At the most he would get two weeks wages, and possibly a chance to get his state redundancy which is a week's wages for every year he's been in the company up to twenty-five years. He was a single lad and his whole life was the shipyard. I couldn't take it in, it was too much. I know I'm soft-hearted, but seeing that lad's face, taking him out of that office and sitting him down and asking him if he was all right was really hard. They were supposed to pick up their gear,

leave the premises straight away and disappear but I sat him down and told him to have a cup of tea. I took the next one in and they said the same thing to him. He had been in the yards for over twenty years and again it was very hard. I then took the next one in. He wasn't too bothered because I think he knew it was coming. He was a shop steward and the company weren't really too keen on shop stewards or they weren't then. So I went back to see the painter and I asked how he was. He had calmed down by then and was going home. I took his address and telephone number. After a week we phoned the lad to see how he was but he wouldn't answer the phone. Then we went round his house but he wouldn't answer. We could hear him crying behind the door.

Mr Chandler

I retired in May 1993, a day on which the company lost the order for the helicopter carrier and two days before they went into receivership. So hitting the age of sixty-five was quite accurately timed but it was very, very sad. I did try to add support to the campaign to save the yard. I wrote to John Major and I spoke on radio.

Hugh Archibold

This is how the *Guardian* reported the start of the crisis at Swan Hunter's in May 1993.

Receivers were yesterday called into Swan Hunter, the stricken Tyneside naval shipyard, amid claims that its collapse had been precipitated by the Ministry of Defence's failure to pay a debt of more than £20 million.

The rapid collapse of the yard into the hands of receivers Price Waterhouse after the loss of a vital order for a Royal Navy helicopter carrier could spell the end of a 120-year tradition of shipbuilding on the Tyne.

The receivers immediately warned that job lay-offs were likely among the yard's 2,200 employees. A further 4,500 jobs among suppliers are also threatened if the yard eventually closes.

A statement by Swan Hunter's four main directors said that the group's financial position meant that there was no alternative to calling in receivers. 'This tragic situation is a bitter blow to a dedicated and superb workforce and design team.' It is understood that the company, bought out by its management in 1986, had an £11 million overdraft facility with Lloyds. The company said that the MoD's failure to pay its claim for £20 million had 'created cash deficit and inability to pay our creditors.'

The company also cited the loss of the carrier contract and the termination of talks with a 'substantial third party', known to have been GEC, the giant defence manufacturer which owns the Yarrow yard on Clydeside. GEC pulled out of takeover talks after the contract was awarded on Tuesday to VSEL, the Trident submarine builder in Barrow, and its projected partner Kvaerner Govan, the Norwegian shipbuilder.

The only substantial work on Swan Hunter's books is the fitting out of three frigates for the Navy. But the crucial £20 million Swan Hunter claims it is owed by the MoD derives from extra work it had to do on the 30,000 tonne fleet replenishment ship *Fort George*.

The MoD has paid £8 million of this but is disputing the rest. 'We feel we have met our contractual obligation to Swan's in full,' a spokesman said yesterday.

Mark Homan, the receivers' senior corporate recovery partner, is to meet the MoD for talks today to see if work on the frigates can be completed and later plans to see the Departments of Employment and Trade and Industry.

'Our wish is to hold together the manufacturing facility together here and the skills while we try to find a buyer for the business,' he said last night.

Wallsend's Labour MP, Stephen Buyers, whose constituency includes the yard, attacked Industry Minister Tim Sainsbury, who on Wednesday announced a £4.5 million aid package for the region, £2 million of which comes from funds set aside as part of the Government's coal closure programme.

Mr Byers said: 'What we had was the spectacle of a Government Minister getting up in the House of Commons and saying he was prepared to allow shipbuilding to die on Tyneside because that is what the market determined. I think that is unacceptable.'

Mr Sainsbury defended the Government stance. 'We are looking backwards to the '70s if we try to say we must keep a shipbuilding yard, a factory or anything else in production regardless of whether anybody is going to buy the product.'

Labour Industry spokesman, Robin Cook, said it was outrageous to describe shipbuilding as an old-fashioned industry. 'We are talking about a hi-tech industry with a highly skilled workforce and the potential to earn sorely needed money for Britain from overseas.'

The Confederation of Shipbuilding Engineering Unions' Campaign Committee in the Wallsend People's Centre.

Labour Party leader, John Smith, visited Swan's to lend his support to the campaign.

The *Evening Chronicle* reported how two young workers were fighting for their jobs:

Two Swan Hunter employees travelled to Downing Street in a bid to safeguard their future.

Amanda Redmond and Ken Gray, both trainees at the threatened yard, helped deliver the second batch of petitions collected through the Save Our Swans Campaign.

Ken, 19, a trainee plumber said: 'It's brilliant the way people in the north-east have rallied round. I never knew so many people cared for the yard. It's a good feeling seeing all these petitions.'

He and Amanda, 18, of Fawdon, Newcastle, were given time off work to personally hand over the forms to No 10.

Trainee electrician Amanda said: 'I like the work, I like the atmosphere and I like the people at Swan Hunter. I don't want it to close.'

Amanda's emotions have ranged from delight at becoming one of 16 young workers taken on last September to despair as she watched 420 colleagues turn up for work only to be told they no longer had jobs.

'That was one of the worst days of my life and I never want to go through it again,' she said.

'There were rumours going round about it for a while, but that didn't prepare us for what happened.

'One day you were joking with people and the next day they weren't there. It was an awful time.

Ken, of Fenham, Newcastle, is uncertain as to what the future holds: 'I'll just take each day as it comes. I never expected Swan's still to be open, so everything now is a bonus.'

In March 1994 Kevin Keegan and Newcastle's first team visited Swan Hunter's to lend their support for the campaign to save the yard. The players helped launch hundreds of balloons with Save Our Swan's postcards attached. Keegan and some of the players expressed their hopes for the future of the stricken yard.

It's important we do anything we can to help. These are difficult times but we must not give up. Swan Hunter and Newcastle United are very much at one with each other. The club went through a bad time but we have turned the corner.

Kevin Keegan

I am a north-east lad. Shipbuilding is a big trade here, they do a good job. It's disappointing what's happened, but hopefully someone else will come forward to buy the yard.

Peter Beardsley

The majority of the workforce here are our supporters. We appreciate that and want to put a little back.

Lee Clark

Life for Swans Campaign

Thanks a million

Thanks to all those who have backed Swan Hunter workers in the first stage of our campaign to save the yard.

Messages and acts of support have flooded in since the company went into receivership.

It is clear that the plight of Swan Hunter has moved the whole of the Northern region and sent some shock waves through the nation.

We believe the political tide has turned as more and more people fear the demise of all our manufacturing industry.

They have seen hundreds of thousand of redundancies in some of our most modern and competitive industries.

Swan's is a shining example of a high-tech, state of the art industry threatened by Government neglect.

Cut out and stick poster... back page

Shipbuilding on the Tyne must remain if our region is to have a manufacturing base on which to reconstruct our economy.

That is why we are not prepared to trade our shipyard for a cut price enterprise zone.

The region needs Swan's, and Swan's needs to build ships.

Welcome to our newsletter

This is the first newsletter of the Life for Swans campaign.

It has been produced by the Confederation of Shipbuilding and Engineering Unions (CSEU) which represents all unions at the yard.

We aim to produce further editions to keep you informed of campaign events as they unfold.

The CSEU is determined to fight to keep shipbuilding on the Tyne.

We actively campaigned to bring the Landing Helicopter Platform order to Swan's, lobbying Parlia-

ment and producing a video promoting the company's excellent track record.

The campaign goes on.

The CSEU needs funds to keep Swan's on the national stage.

Anyone who wants to contribute to the fighting fund should make cheques payable to the

Swan Hunter Co-ordinating Committee at Wallsend People's Centre, 10, Frank Street, Wallsend. Tyne and Wear

Campaign Newsletter No1, June 1993. Published by Swan Hunter CSEU, Representing all Shipyard Trades Unions

Bit by bit the workforce was made redundant. Hundreds of workers left an industry that many had been in for years. One letter to the *Journal*, from December 1993, summed up the feeling of Swan Hunter's employees at that time.

Last Monday, November 29, saw a further reduction in our already depleted workforce here at Swan's, another traumatic blow to our morale.

This has lowered our numbers to about 1,000 employees, Five hundred people were made redundant, a third of the people we had left. There was no alternative to this, due to lack of new work, and due to no fault of their own these people were cast out to a life of untold worry, stress and in some cases utter despair.

When one's livelihood is removed, and one's income is chopped off, especially at this time of year, it must be very distressing to say the least. I, along with all of us left here, at Swan's want you all to know you are in our thoughts.

Last Monday was a horrific day here, no-one knew who was going, and until it actually happened everyone was living in hope that it would not be them.

Those of us who are left feel really sorry and totally devastated to lose our friends in this way, comrades, people we have known for years and years in some cases. We shall always remember them.

At the moment we have 1,000 highly-skilled people left on the books, 1,000 representatives of the many thousands of Tyneside's best, the salt of the earth, men and women whose jobs have been lost.

Swan Hunter on Tyneside are the champions at shipbuilding. We cannot be beaten on product, quality, time in building, or workmanship. Our design team and our management are the best. We have agreements second to none. We have the knowledge and the expertise, we have proven this time and time again.

We continue to produce the very best warships for our customer, the MoD. Given the opportunity of intervention funding we will recover and we here at Swan Hunter will show the world once more what we are capable of.

Bill Kell
Swan Hunter

SWAN HUNTER

IF THERE IS ANOTHER

ROUND OF JOB LOSSES

AT SWAN HUNTER,

HOW FAR WILL THE

RIPPLES SPREAD?

Life for Swans

There are two types of swans in Britain.
One is protected by the Crown.
The other faces extinction.
The Swan's we're talking about build ships on the Tyne.

Swan Hunter shipbuilders are in the hands of the receiver.
It is a high-tech, high-skill industry.
And Swan's forms the bedrock of our manufacturing industry.

It will be a keystone in rebuilding our economy.

6,000 jobs depend on Swan's.

We cannot afford to let them go under.

Swan's needs a vote of confidence and immediate help from the Government.

The North East, and Britain, need our manufacturing.

We need Swan's on our river.

Published by Swan Hunter CSEU

The *News Guardian* marked the leaving of the last ship at the yard, HMS *Richmond*, in November 1994:

Tears and silence as Richmond slips away
'Being the best simply wasn't enough'

They promised to fight on to keep shipbuilding alive on the Tyne, but it still felt like a funeral as HMS *Richmond* slipped almost guiltily away from Swan Hunter's dockyard and on to the grey murk of a wet and miserable November day.

Hundreds of workers, past and present and their families watched her go, almost in silence, many too choked to speak, much less cheer the departure of the last ship to leave Swan's.

The best they managed was a round of applause as the ship's crew, standing smartly to attention down the side of the ship, saluted the yard and its workers with three ceremonial waves of their white caps on each of three cheers.

Richmond's captain, Commander Andrew Underwood, said the quality of the workmanship was of the highest standard. Around 50 of her crew have worked alongside yard employees for the last 15 months as the ship was completed.

The Swan Hunter's band.

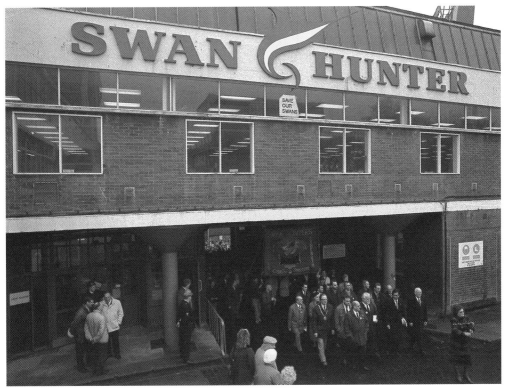

A Northumbrian piper leads out the workforce on the day HMS *Richmond* left the yard.

'It is a very emotional day for us too. We have very mixed feelings and our thoughts go out to all the workforce, many of whom have become confirmed friends.'

The *Richmond* has set new production records on sea trials. But as Swan's public relations consultant Robin Ashby said when the yard first plunged into receivership 18 months ago, being the best simply wasn't good enough.

And as the Swan Hunter brass band played *Auld Lang Syne*, the people of Wallsend, many in tears, watched their livelihoods float away, straining to keep the *Richmond* in sight as long as possible.

Many of them remembered the days when Swan's ships towered over terraced streets, when the yard's hooter regulated the life of everyone in the town.

Then the *Richmond* was gone, nothing blocking the view across the river; a yard which had once rung to the sound of rivets finally eerily silent.

Sold Down The River
by Tony Parker

Hammers ring across the yard,
in the shadow of cranes the work is hard.
They build the ships and win the fame,
for the yard that bears Swan Hunter's name.

Highly skilled and second to none,
so where have all the workers gone,
welders, burners, fitters and all,
have been selected for a fall.

Sent up the bank with a box of tools,
each one a victim of ignorant fools.
A giro cheque the only compensation,
life on the dole in sheer frustration.

They want to work and earn their pay,
now the fools have blown it away.
Out on the stones they can't earn a crust,
they want to be back in the metal and dust.

They build the ships and they are proud,
they don't want to rot in the giro shroud.
It costs more to keep them outside the yard,
leave them some dignity it can't be hard.

If the shipyard is destined to die,
'Who is to blame' the people will cry.
It wasn't the workers we know it's a fact,
it was the Government dogma and failure to act.

It's always seemed to me that shipbuilding is not so much a job, but a way of life. Although it has its peculiar and difficult moments from time to time, it also has its recompenses. I sometimes cheer myself up in the darker moments by saying it could have been so much worse. I could have worked in a dog-meat factory or a car factory and then I wouldn't have had the satisfaction of knowing that the result of your endeavours are those lovely creatures that go up and down the river from time to time.

Albert Buckton

THE PRIDE OF
THE TYNE

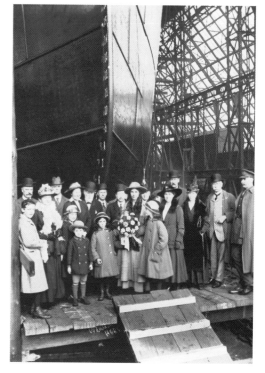

125

Can You Help?

The People's History is planning further volumes of 'Shipyard Stories' and is interested to hear from anyone who would like to contribute. If you have any tales of the shipyards of the Tyne or the Wear please write to:

> Andrew Clark
> The People's History
> Suite 1
> Byron House
> Seaham Grange Business Park
> Seaham
> County Durham
> SR7 0PY

The People's History

To find out more about this unique series of local history books – and to
receive a catalogue of the latest titles – send a large stamped addressed
envelope to:

The People's History Ltd
Suite 1
Byron House
Seaham Grange Business Park
Seaham
County Durham
SR7 0PY